THE RIVER SEVERN
A Pictorial History

from Shrewsbury to Gloucester

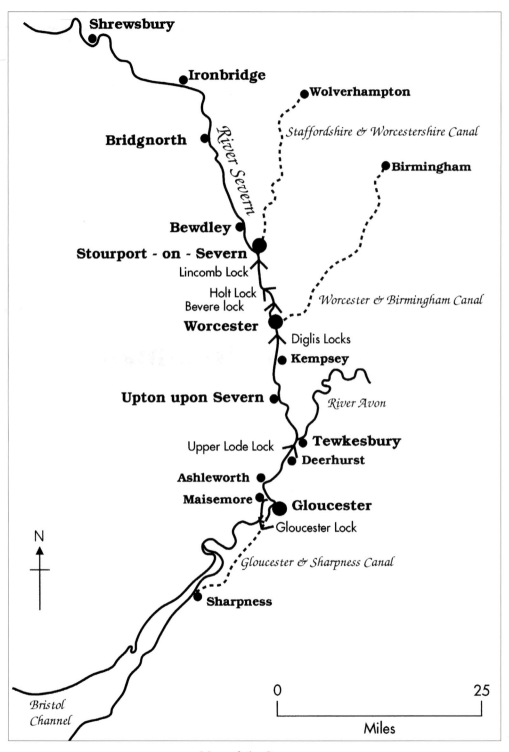

Map of the Severn

THE RIVER SEVERN
A Pictorial History

from Shrewsbury to Gloucester

Josephine Jeremiah

Phillimore

1998

Published by
PHILLIMORE & CO. LTD.,
Shopwyke Manor Barn, Chichester, West Sussex

ISBN 0 85033 985 5

Printed and bound in Great Britain by
BIDDLES LTD.
Guildford, Surrey

List of Illustrations

Frontispiece: Map of the Severn

Acknowledgements

My thanks go to The Shropshire Records and Research Centre for giving permission for the reproduction of illustrations 18 and 19, to the Ironbridge Gorge Museum Trust for illustrations 32, 33 and 34, to Mrs. E. Bent for illustration 127 and to the Almonry Heritage Centre, Evesham for illustration 144.

I would particularly like to thank my husband, Ian Jeremiah, for his research and help in selecting material for this book.

In memory of my nephew
Ewart David Lowe 1966-1998

Introduction

The River Severn, at around 220 miles in length, is Britain's longest river. It rises on the slopes of Plynlimon, in Wales, and passes through the Welsh towns of Llanidloes, Newtown and Welshpool before reaching Shrewsbury, the first English town on the river. Known as the 'King's high stream of Severn', meaning that it was free with no toll to be paid, the river was a principal trade route from medieval times. Up to the second half of the 16th century, downstream cargoes included wool, hides and grain while luxury commodities such as wine and foreign goods were brought upriver from Bristol. In 1570, the first boat carried coal downriver from Ironbridge and, from then on, trade in coal expanded. The main inland ports were Bridgnorth, Bewdley, Worcester and Gloucester but there were many quays, not only in the cities and towns but near the villages, too, as isolated communities depended on supplies brought by river. By the end of the 17th century, the Severn was busier than any other European river, except for the Meuse. It was an important link with the coal mines and ironworks of Shropshire during the 18th century and by the end of that century, via the canal system, with the industrial Midlands.

According to the *Gentleman's Magazine* (1758), the traffic on the Severn was carried on with vessels of two sorts: 'the lesser kind are called barges and frigates, being from 40 to 60 feet in length, have a single mast, square sail, and carry from 20 to 40 tons; the trows, or larger vessels, are from 40 to 80 tons burthen; these have a main and top mast, about 80 feet high, with square sails, and some have mizen masts; they are generally from 16 to 20 feet wide and 60 in length'. In May 1756, a list of barges and trows belonging to different places on the Severn had been compiled and this was published in the magazine, the numbers adding up to 376 vessels.

Barges and frigates were upriver trows which only worked on the river above Gloucester. They had open, saucer-shaped, shallow-draughted hulls to enable them to work in the shallow waters of the upper river. Craft could once be taken as far as Pool Quay, below Welshpool, but there were considerable difficulties in navigation on the upper stretches because of the summer shortage of water and shoals across the river. Using the river's flow and their sails on downriver journeys, trows were pulled upstream against the current by bow-hauliers in teams of up to twenty men who were harnessed to a towing-rope. The work must have been extremely hard but the bow-hauliers strongly resisted attempts to introduce horses for towing though eventually, by 1812, a towing-path for horses stretched from Shrewsbury to Gloucester.

The larger trows operated on the Severn estuary and the Bristol Channel as well as the lower reaches of the river. These flat-bottomed craft mostly had distinctive, 'D'-shaped transom sterns and deeper hulls than the smaller upriver trows. Originally square-rigged, many of them were converted to smack or ketch rig in the 19th century, to enable them to trade further out into the Bristol Channel as competition on the river from tugs and barges forced them to seek cargoes from further afield.

At **Shrewsbury**, quays were established at Mardol, by the Welsh Bridge, and on the opposite side of the river at Frankwell. Another quay for the loading and unloading of merchandise was by the English Bridge. Walking along Shrewsbury's delightful riverside walk today, it is hard to imagine that, in 1756, the town owned 19 trading vessels. Boats were also built here, a late example being the steam tug, launched in 1858, which assisted in the construction of the Severn Valley Railway, the line that was to help bring about the demise of the river trade. Until the railway bridge was built in the mid-19th century, only two bridges, the Welsh Bridge and the English Bridge, crossed the Severn at Shrewsbury. Now, a number of bridges cross the river as it loops around the town.

Past Shrewsbury, the river turns north to **Ditherington**, the location of a one-time, flax-spinning mill which was the world's first iron-framed building. Here, the Severn changes to an easterly direction for **Uffington** and is followed by the course of the long-disused Shrewsbury Canal. Uffington, which once possessed its own canal wharf and crane, is situated between the river and the old canal. Today, the wharfside cottages are a reminder of the former waterway. In past days, Shrewsbury folk would cross the river from Monkmoor by Uffington ferry to reach the village's riverside inn where there was a bowling green and quoit yard. A favourite walk was to the impressive ruins of Haughmond Abbey and the summit of Haughmond Hill, both not far from the village. Near the abbey, the Battle of Shrewsbury was fought in 1403 between Henry IV and the Percies, the king being the victor.

From Uffington, the river takes a southerly course and is crossed, near **Preston Boats**, by the fine, cast-iron Belvidere Bridge carrying the railway. At Preston Boats, a rope ferry used to operate above the ancient fish-weir which was built across the river on osier-covered islands. The fish-weir once belonged to the Haughmond monks and was still in use during the early years of the 20th century, the eels caught being much relished by the local populace.

Downstream of Preston Boats are the estates of the secluded **Longner Hall**, built in 1803 by John Nash, and the imposing **Attingham Park**, designed by the architect, George Steuart, who incorporated the original house, Tern Hall, into the late 18th-century building. An unusual feature of the latter is that Steuart planned a set of rooms for males on one side of the entrance hall and a similar set for females on the other side. In the early 19th century, a picture gallery was built by Nash for the art-collector, the 2nd Lord Berwick.

At nearby **Atcham**, the Severn flows beneath two bridges. The older, 18th-century bridge was well-used by stage-coaches travelling between the ferry port of Holyhead and London. Modern traffic crosses by the newer, 1920s bridge and the old bridge has for many years been the home of a colony of house martins whose nests have blended into its stonework. Near the bridges is the *Mytton and Mermaid Hotel* which commemorates the name of Mad Jack Mytton, an eccentric, early 19th-century squire. Born to wealth, he drank and gambled away his fortune yet remained a popular figure, many tales of his wild behaviour being handed down in local folklore.

The River Tern passes through Attingham's parkland before joining the Severn midway between Atcham and Wroxeter. Near the latter are located the ruins of **Viroconium**. Originally a fort situated at a strategic point on the east bank of the Severn, it became the fourth largest town in Roman Britain and the capital of the Cornovii tribe. Among the remains is the bath area where a high section of the bath wall is known as the 'Old Work'. The church of St Andrew in **Wroxeter**, like St Eata's Church in Atcham, has stone from the Roman site in its construction.

The stretch of the river down to Buildwas has great appeal, with the Wrekin on one side and Wenlock Edge on the other. Some distance downriver of Wroxeter, the Cound Brook enters the Severn on its western bank. **Cound** must have been of some importance on the Severn in days gone by. In 1756, Cound and Buildwas, between them, had seven vessels trading on the river. No doubt, *Cound Lodge Inn*, standing on the river, benefited from the heyday of the river trade. Years later, when 'Quaestor', (W. Byford-Jones), stayed at the inn, things were much quieter. 'Quaestor', who wrote articles for the *Express & Star*, Wolverhampton, recounted his visit in a chapter entitled 'Christmas Peace on Severn' in *Midland Leaves* (1934).

There was no bridge across the Severn between Atcham and Buildwas until Thomas Telford built a wooden toll-bridge at **Cressage** in the late 18th century. This was succeeded by a structure of reinforced concrete, built in 1913. Cressage is said to mean Christ's Oak and it is traditionally held that St Augustine met Welsh priests under an oak tree, here, though several places along the Severn make a similar claim. After Cressage, the sides of the valley start to close in. The Severn passes the village of **Leighton**, the birthplace of the novelist, Mary Webb, and flows under Leighton Bank, from the top of which are striking views of the river meandering in the valley below. Soon **Buildwas** is reached, the village on one side of the river and the ruins of Buildwas Abbey on the other, a modern bridge linking the two. Buildwas Abbey was founded in 1135 for monks of the Savigny order. Taken over by the Cistercians 12 years later, it became a centre of commerce, controlling much land. The monks used the river to transport wool, from their large flocks of sheep, to Bristol from where it was sent to France. The remains of the abbey church and, in particular, the vaulted chapter house with its medieval floor tiles are memorable, the peaceful setting being very different from the huge, cooling towers of the power station nearby.

The Ironbridge Gorge, formed during the last Ice Age, is a very great contrast to the flat water-meadows through which the Severn has previously been flowing. Here, among the steep wooded slopes, are **Ironbridge** and **Coalbrookdale**. Often labelled the 'Cradle of the Industrial Revolution', the area has a superb range of historical industrial sites which attract many visitors. It was at Coalbrookdale, in 1708, that Abraham Darby of Bristol took over the ironworks and founded the famous Coalbrookdale Company. The iron ore, wood and limestone used in the production of iron were to be found in the locality but there was another raw material, coal, which was to prove a vital resource. Darby discovered that, by using coke instead of charcoal to smelt iron, goods could be made more cheaply and iron production was no longer dependent on the country's diminishing stocks of timber. The company's three-legged, cast-iron cooking pots became well-known all over the world and Coalbrookdale became famous as the place where the world's first iron bridge was cast and where the boiler for the world's first locomotive was made.

There was no bridge between Buildwas and Bridgnorth before the Iron Bridge was erected. It was constructed in cast iron between 1777 and 1779 and officially opened on 1 January 1781. At the outset, a Shrewsbury architect, Thomas Farnolls Pritchard, was involved in its design though he died in 1777. The work went ahead under the direction of Abraham Darby III who financed much of the £5,000 needed to build the bridge. Anyone using the bridge had to pay a toll. The highest charge was two shillings for a carriage drawn by six horses while the lowest was one halfpenny for a calf, pig, sheep, lamb or pedestrian.

Coracles used to be kept along the river at Ironbridge to save the cost of crossing the bridge. They had a light framework of ash laths, woven into a bowl shape. Originally covered with hide, unbleached calico was used later and a waterproof covering made by coating the coracles with a mixture of pitch and tar. Ironbridge coracles were different from the Shrewsbury and Welshpool coracles, being broader and more easily handled. They were almost oval and measured around 57 inches in length and about 36 inches in width. Besides being needed for ferrying, they were also used for poaching. Brian Waters, in *Severn Stream* (1949), devoted half a chapter to amusing reminiscences concerning the Ironbridge poachers who supported about twelve families, at the beginning of the 20th century, by illegally taking rabbits and game.

These cockle-shell boats were not the only craft to be constructed in the gorge during past days. In 1756, 139 vessels altogether were owned at **Madeley Wood**, **Benthall** and **Broseley** and many of these boats were built locally, one boat-building site being the Bower Yard on the Benthall bank. Boat-building flourished because the development of coal mining and iron working, in the vicinity, led to an increase of traffic on the Severn during the 18th century. From 1760, over 100,000 tons of coal were transported each year, by river, from mines around Broseley and Madeley while, besides iron ore and iron goods, boats also carried bricks, tiles, pottery and the famous Broseley clay pipes.

River craft were also built downriver of Ironbridge at **Jackfield**, once the home of Severn watermen and well-known for the decorative tiles produced by Maw & Co. and Messrs. Craven, Dunnill & Co. Workers from Jackfield used the Coalport ferry to get to the Coalport China Works on the opposite side of the river. This ferry capsized and sank on the night of 23 October 1799 and 28 people were drowned, among them some of the works' most highly-skilled hands. John Randall recorded the incident in *The Clay Industries including the Fictile and Ceramic Arts on the Banks of the Severn* (1877): 'It was a dark night, the boat was crowded, and the man at the helm, not having been accustomed to put the boat over allowed the vessel to swing around in the channel where, with a strong tide running, it was drawn under by the rope which went from the mast to a rock in the bed of the river'.

The Coalport ferry was eventually replaced by the Jackfield War Memorial Bridge, built for pedestrians in 1922. Two other bridges are in the vicinity, the new Jackfield Free Bridge, constructed in 1994 on the site of the old bridge which opened in 1909, and Coalport Bridge. The original bridge at **Coalport** was built of timber in 1777 but it was seriously damaged by the 1795 flood. Rebuilt as a single span, using iron ribs and a timber deck, the whole bridge was eventually converted to iron in 1818. On the left bank of the river, between the Jackfield footbridge and Coalport Bridge, is the Hay Inclined Plane, linking the Shropshire Canal with a canal parallel to the river at Coalport. Tub boats, carrying goods, were once raised and lowered here.

A short distance after Coalport, though still flowing slightly to the east, the Severn changes to a more southerly direction and more or less keeps to this course until Tewkesbury is reached. Between Coalport and Bridgnorth, the wood-fringed river is secluded and little known. On the eastern bank is **Apley Park** with its castellated Gothic mansion. In Victorian times visitors were allowed to visit the park and Apley Terrace, a wooded height overlooking the Severn though, according to John Randall in *The*

Tourist's Guide to Bridgnorth (1875), 'some limit has been necessary to stop bull-dog owners and mischievous revellers who here, as elsewhere, have done all they could to close such places to the public'. Apley Park Bridge, a private suspension bridge over the river, was built in 1909 and connected the estate with Linley station on the Severn Valley Railway.

Bridgnorth is in an outstanding setting with High Town elevated on a sandstone ridge above the Severn and Low Town below the cliff and across the river. For hundreds of years, the river was of great importance to the town and, by the 18th century, this was a lively river port with many boats trading up and down the Severn calling here. Passengers and goods were landed at the old quay by the bridge-foot, the river craft being brought alongside the quay by horses working a big wooden pulley. Near the quay were some commodious warehouses where merchandise could be stored. Bridgnorth itself had 75 barges and trows in 1756, the vessels being owned by 47 different individuals. There were also boat-building yards along this stretch of the river and not only river craft were built at Bridgnorth; on occasion sea-going vessels were constructed here, too.

A boat-building yard was once situated on the eastern bank of the river at **Quatford**, downriver of Bridgnorth. John Smalman is credited with building a small look-out tower above this establishment. He also erected the 19th-century, castellated mansion on the hillside though the site of the original motte-and-bailey Norman castle is on a rocky bank nearer to the river. High above the Severn is the church of St Mary Magdalene. Parishioners from **Eardington**, across the river, used the Quatford ferry when they attended church. A.G. Bradley, in *The Book of the Severn* (1920), reported a conversation he had with the ferryman who was also the sexton of the church. The latter bemoaned the passing of the barge trade as hardly a rowing boat came by to cheer him up. After the cessation of barge traffic, the crossing had become a rope ferry. Brian Waters, in *Severn Stream*, recorded that it was the scene of a fatal accident when a honeymoon couple, on a rowing holiday downstream, were caught by the rope and drowned.

The river, having turned east towards the cliff topped by Quatford church, now resumes its southerly course past the landscaped parkland of **Dudmaston Hall**. At **Hampton Loade** there is a station on the preserved Severn Valley Railway and a cable-ferry. The latter operates using a cable which crosses the river between two supports. The ferry-boat is connected to it by another cable which slides along it, the ferryman using the current against the boat's rudder to move the craft from bank to bank. Writing about this crossing, in the 1930s, in *Both Sides of the Severn*, 'Quaestor' noted that the fare was three halfpence for foot passengers while it cost 6d. for a cow and 2d. for a sheep or calf. The author thought that none of those would have enjoyed the passage a quarter as much as he did!

Downriver from Hampton Loade, the river banks become steeper. The Alveley and Highley collieries used to be situated on either side of the river but the land has been reclaimed and now forms the **Severn Valley Country Park**. Pedestrians use the concrete Alveley Colliery Bridge which links the two former mine sites. The parish of **Alveley** is on the eastern bank of the Severn and that of **Highley** is on the western bank. Both villages are situated on higher ground above the river, Highley having terraced miners' cottages while Alveley has more rural features. John Randall, in *The Tourist's Guide to Bridgnorth*, commented on the ferry crossing which once linked the two communities: 'From Highley you cross by a boat at Stanley, and the chances are you will be paddled across by as fair a country maiden as you may wish to see, a circumstance compensating, in some degree, for the inconvenience of the path past Little London, a place so completely the antipodes of anything the name suggests that it is a wonder how it could have been applied'.

Another ferry was at **Upper Arley**, where a large vessel was capable of transporting vehicles as well as foot passengers. After the closure of the ferry in the 1960s, a footbridge was built in 1971 and this connects the village with Arley station on the Severn Valley Railway. Past Upper Arley, the cast-iron Victoria Bridge takes the railway line across the river. Eyemore Wood is on high ground on the east side while Seckley Wood, part of Wyre Forest, comes down to the water on the western bank. Between Arley and Bewdley there were a number of fords which must have made navigation difficult at times of low water. Writing in the late 19th century, George Thompson, in *Country Rambles Round Kidderminster*, named these fords as The Seckley, White Horses, The Falley, Roundstone, Halfpenny, Bridewell and Dowles, commenting that The Falley, meaning 'the fall near the island', was wrongly named Folly, even on Ordnance maps.

The Severn has played a prominent part in the history of **Bewdley**. In centuries past, there was much river traffic here and at **Wribbenhall** on the opposite bank. Trade was well-established by 1412, when the men of Bewdley are said to have been bold watermen who owned large barges or trows. An old story has it that they would not allow any carriage of goods on the river past Bewdley unless it was conveyed by their own craft, which resulted in Bristol and Gloucester petitioning Parliament that Bewdley might be passed without hindrance. Over the years, these watermen were noted as having the best boats and best crews on the river. Bewdley's carrying trade was so successful that Bristol merchants set up depots for their merchandise on both sides of the river and Bewdley became an important distribution centre. Goods were carried from the town by trains of laden pack-horses which returned with more commodities to be shipped out. This accounts for the large number of inns with accommodation for horses in the locality. If the junction with the Staffordshire & Worcestershire Canal had been established here, instead of four miles downriver, then Bewdley might have continued to thrive. In the event, the townsfolk were against the proposal and the creation in the late 18th century of a new canal town at Stourport-on-Severn helped to bring about the demise of Bewdley's river trade.

Below Bewdley, the Severn curves around an outcrop of red sandstone rock on its east bank. This is named **Blackstone Rock**, possibly because of the lichens encrusting it. Blackstone was the location of an ancient ford. In *The Severn Valley* (1882), John Randall mentioned being 'imprisoned for the night on board a barge which grounded on the rocks' at the ford, though the next morning he was 'highly pleased with the beauty and novelty of the scene'. **Ribbesford**, with its church and the turreted Ribbesford House, lies on the opposite side of the river and the steep hillside on the west bank is covered by Ribbesford Woods almost down to Stourport, the bare top of Stagborough Hill standing above the woods.

Within a few years of the establishment of the junction of the Staffordshire & Worcestershire Canal with the Severn in 1772, a little hamlet near the mouth of the River Stour became the busy inland port of **Stourport-on-Severn**. Here, canal basins were dug out and two sets of locks constructed, one for canal narrowboats and the other for broader river craft. Wharves were built and warehouses erected for the storage of merchandise, notable among the canal buildings being the former warehouse with its distinctive clocktower in the 'Clock' basin and the prominent *Tontine Hotel*, once the setting of many a grand social function. Although, after the coming of the railways, river and canal trade eventually declined at Stourport, by the early years of the century its waterfront was often bustling with day trippers, some of whom took excursions on the river's pleasure steamers. Today, the town is still a popular resort with visitors from the surrounding area while others from further afield use the river and canal for holiday boating trips.

Downriver from Stourport, the high **Redstone Rock** rises from the west bank. Well-known in past times for its hermitage, there was once a ferry and ford at this location. George Thompson, in *Country Rambles Round Kidderminster*, wrote: 'Waggons crossed by the ford, when the river was sufficiently low, until the dredging of the bed of the river up to Stourport Locks rendered the ford impassable. Opposite the ferry-house may be seen the remains of the old landing-stage, and near it another house, formerly the Cross Inn, whence a road led to the foot of the sand-dunes on Hartlebury Common, and so on to Worcester'.

Lincomb Lock, in its wooded setting a short distance downstream, is the highest lock on the Severn. Its construction and that of Lincomb weir was part of the mid-19th-century improvements to the river between Stourport and Gloucester. At **The Burf**, half a mile below the lock, is *Hampstall Inn*, at one time a cider house and the site of a ferry. Mrs. Berkeley, in her paper on 'The Ferries of Worcestershire' (1931), noted that 'the old track by the Burf was the direct way from Abberley Pass to Hartlebury and Dudley'. The ferry has long gone but the inn still caters for boats on the river with customer moorings and a riverside garden.

The Severn flows on past **Shrawley Wood**, the northern edge of which is bounded by Dick Brook. In the 17th century, this narrow stream was made navigable by Andrew Yarranton, who built two flash locks near its junction with the Severn. Iron was taken along the brook to a forge above the upper lock. Shrawley Wood is an ancient, primary woodland renowned for its small-leaved lime trees, which at one time were cut as coppice wood, loaded into narrowboats at nearby Lenchford wharf and sent to the Potteries for the making of crates. Alders were also utilised. Every year clogmakers would camp out in Shrawley Wood and cut the alderwood which was made into soles for clogs.

Below **Holt Lock**, the handsome Holt Fleet Bridge leads to **Ombersley**, a picturesque village with black-and-white cottages, situated some distance from the river. **Holt Fleet**, with its riverside inn, was a magnet for day trippers in the days of the pleasure steamers, excursions being run from Stourport, Worcester and Tewkesbury. Downstream of the bridge there are no riverside communities until Worcester is reached, **Grimley** and **Hallow** being set back from the west bank and **Bevere** and **Northwick** from the east side of the river.

Before the building of Bevere weir in the 1840s, there was a river crossing at Hawford just above the junction of the River Salwarpe with the Severn. In the words of Mrs. Berkeley: 'It was called Rovin ferry, and by its means horses and even vehicles could be ferried across the river'. The ferry was situated in this spot because here the towing-path changed from the west to the east side of the Severn. The River Salwarpe joins the Severn accompanied by the disused Droitwich Barge Canal, which was busy in the 19th century with the Droitwich salt trade. A little way downriver is **Bevere Lock**, once known as Camp Lock and now, with its flower garden, one of the best-kept locks on the waterways.

For centuries, **Worcester** was a main port of call for the river trade and, in days gone by, the waterfront must have been a lively place with craft loading and unloading. Reputed to have been the haunt of smugglers, there were bustling, watermen's inns and a warren of narrow alleyways beside the river. The birth of the Industrial Revolution brought cargoes of coal and iron from Shropshire which helped business to flourish. Furthermore, the canal links of the Staffordshire & Worcestershire Canal, opened in 1772, and the completion of the Worcestershire & Birmingham Canal in 1815, meant growth of trade with the Midlands. Goods were transhipped at the canal basins in Worcester, Diglis Basin handling wine and grain plus other commodities while Lowesmoor Basin dealt in timber and coal. The canal narrowboats, or 'longboats' as they were known on the Severn, were drawn by horses at first. Later on, tugs, each towing a line of narrowboats, became a familiar sight on the river. However, despite the l9th-century improvements to the Severn, the arrival of Worcester's railway in 1850 heralded the decline in both river and canal trade. From the late 1920s up until the 1960s, commercial traffic was revived with tankers carrying petroleum upriver to Worcester and Stourport but, since the closure of the oil wharves, craft passing through Worcester have been mainly pleasure boats.

South of Worcester, the River Teme flows into the Severn on its west bank, the site of the 1651 Battle of Worcester, the last battle of the Civil War. At **Kempsey**, the church of St Mary the Virgin stands on rising ground overlooking the river and there is a fine view of the Malverns from the Ham. Kempsey was a manor belonging to Walter Cantilupe, Bishop of Worcester, and it was here that Simon de Montfort and his captive, Henry III, stayed on the night of 2 August 1265, having crossed the Severn with his army, two days prior to the Battle of Evesham. Pixham ferry once operated from the *Pixham Ferry Inn* to the Kempsey bank. The inn closed down in 1903 but the ferry continued to be worked for many years. There were also ferries at **Clevelode** and the **Rhydd**. Clevelode ferry was still working when Mrs. Berkeley researched Worcestershire ferries in the early 1930s, though it seems to have gone out of operation by 1939. The ferry at the Rhydd, described by John Randall in *The Severn Valley* as the Great Malvern ferry, is thought to have been in existence up to the First World War.

Another tall, red sandstone outcrop is at the Rhydd and a rock bar across the river here was a hazard to navigation before the improvements to the waterway. At the top of the cliff, but hidden from the river, is the 19th-century **Rhydd Court**, converted into a hospital during the First World War and now known as Cliffey House School. Two other large houses can be seen from the river. The imposing **Severn Bank**, near the black-and-white village of **Severn Stoke**, is situated on the east bank while the Lechmere mansion, **Severn End**, lies on the west bank not far from the village of **Hanley Castle**. The castle has long gone from the latter and the quay at the end of the lane from the village is no more.

Nearby **Upton upon Severn**'s quayside was busy in days gone by, as the riverside town was an inland port serving neighbouring Herefordshire. In medieval times, the Bishop of Hereford purchased foreign wine at Bristol and had it sent up the Severn to Upton from where it was taken overland to his favourite residence at Bosbury. John

Randall in *The Severn Valley* observed: 'From its position upon the Severn, and its being the centre of a fruit-producing county, Upton is the great depot for cider which is brought down to its wharf and shipped to all parts of England'. The waterfront at Upton is still busy but the moorings are now taken up by pleasure craft.

Leaving Upton, the river flows past the site of a former ferry at **Saxon's Lode** and a little further on past the location of the Uckinghall or Ripple ferry where all that remains are the ferry steps down to the water. The neighbouring villages of **Uckinghall** and **Ripple** are situated on the east bank of the Severn though not on the riverside. The latter is celebrated for the medieval misericord carvings in St Mary's Church which show seasonal occupations like hedging, sowing and harvesting. In Ripple churchyard is the 'Giant's Grave' belonging to Robert Reeve, reputed to have been over 7ft. tall, who died, in 1626, after mowing the 100-acre Uckinghall meadow for a bet.

The river glides on towards Tewkesbury, its high banks tree-covered with only the traffic on the M50 road bridge disturbing its isolation. Before Thomas Telford's Mythe Bridge is reached, the steep wooded cliff of the Mythe rises from the eastern bank. It's said that boatmen on narrowboats used to fill their water cans at a spot just above the bridge as springs in the river bed there made the water very clean. The Severn-Trent waterworks are adjacent to the bridge. Soon after, the Severn is entered by the Warwickshire Avon, the lock connecting the two waterways being a short distance from the confluence. Downriver from Tewkesbury is the huge **Upper Lode Lock**, capable of taking a steam tug and her numerous barges. Another channel of the Avon, the Mill Avon, joins the Severn at Lower Lode, thus enclosing a great water-meadow, the Severn Ham, between the town of **Tewkesbury** and the Severn. When the river is at normal level it can not be seen from the town but at times of flood the Ham is covered with water and Tewkesbury can almost be turned into an island.

The fine, square tower of Tewkesbury Abbey dominates the town. Founded by Robert Fitzhamon after the Norman Conquest, the building was continued under the patronage of his son-in-law, Robert Fitzroy, Earl of Gloucester, the abbey being consecrated in 1121. Stone for the tower is said to have been brought by sea from Caen in Normandy and then up the Severn to Tewkesbury. Other prominent patrons were the de Clares, Despensers and Beauchamps, and their tombs and chantry chapels are impressive features of the building. After Tewkesbury Abbey was dissolved in 1540, the Benedictine monastery was pulled down but the townsfolk were allowed to buy the abbey church as it was their parish church. Fortunately for future generations, they were able to come up with the £453 which was an estimate for the value of the lead on the roof and the metal of the bells.

Besides being distinguished for its splendid abbey, its half-timbered houses and its fascinating alleyways, Tewkesbury is also known for its battle on 4 May 1471. Prior to the combat, Queen Margaret of Anjou and her Lancastrian forces, prevented from crossing the Severn at Gloucester, had hoped to use the Lower Lode crossing but they arrived too exhausted to make the attempt. The Battle of Tewkesbury took place on a nearby field, since known as the 'Bloody Meadow', and ended with the Yorkists defeating the Lancastrians.

Looking upriver from **Lower Lode**, there is a spectacular view of Tewkesbury Abbey with Bredon Hill in the distance. Downstream of Lower Lode, the tower of the Saxon church of St Mary at **Deerhurst** can be seen from the river. Another notable Saxon building, Odda's Chapel, is nearby. Opposite Deerhurst, the village of **Chaceley** lies back from the west bank of the river, though the *Yew Tree Inn* stands on the riverside at Chaceley Stock. This one-time cider house used to cater for the needs of the rivermen but is now patronised by members of the sailing club based here and by pleasure boaters for whom moorings are provided. There are a number of other waterside inns downstream including the *Coal House*, once known as the *White Lion Inn*, at Apperley, the *Haw Bridge Inn* and the *New Inn* on the Tirley side at Haw Bridge, the *Red Lion Inn* at Wainlode and the *Boat* at Ashleworth Quay. The villages of **Apperley** and **Tirley**, situated on opposite sides of the river, are linked by Haw Bridge, built in 1961 to replace the original 1825 bridge demolished by a tanker barge. Other villages like **Hasfield**, on the west side of the river, and **Leigh**, on the east, lie well back from the flood plain.

For centuries, the Severnside communities, downriver of Tewkesbury, have been involved in elver fishing. Elvers are young eels, about three inches long, which come up the Severn during March and April, having travelled in long eel-fares from their spawning grounds in the Atlantic Ocean. Elver fishing is usually carried on at night, during the spring tides, a lantern drawing the elvers to the box-like net which is dipped into the river at the turn of the tide. The net is submerged for one or two minutes before being raised and the elvers poured into a bucket. Local folk have long regarded elvers as a delicacy, cooking them in bacon fat whereupon they turn from being translucent to milky-white.

Between Haw Bridge and **Wainlode Hill** is the entrance to the disused Coombe Hill Canal which was originally planned to supply Cheltenham with coal though the canal never reached there, being abandoned in 1876. Past Wainlode's high cliff, the next settlement is **Ashleworth**, where a captivating group of medieval buildings, including the church, tithe barn and Ashleworth Court, is located behind the riverside inn on the quay. The large Ashleworth horse ferry was important in the days of horse-drawn boat traffic, as the towing-path changed sides here in order to avoid Wainlode Hill and tributaries to the Severn such as the Chelt and the Avon. A tale of the former ferry was recounted by Brian Waters in *Severn Tide* (1947), and concerned the occasion when a fox swam across the river and the whole hunt packed on to the ferry demanding to be taken over at one go. To avert a disaster, the ferryman ordered the 30 horsemen off and relayed smaller numbers across while other members swam their horses to the other side. It was not noted whether the fox escaped during this frantic interlude.

The stretch of water below Ashleworth to the Upper Parting is known as Long Reach. At the Upper Parting, the Severn divides into two channels around the low-lying Alney Island. A short distance along the west channel is the disused Maisemore Lock. This channel, which goes past the village of **Maisemore**, is now unnavigable. In past times, it was used for access to the Herefordshire & Gloucestershire Canal whose junction with the Severn was near **Gloucester**. The navigable east channel takes the river into Gloucester under a series of road and railway bridges before the old quayside and Gloucester Lock, the entrance to Gloucester Docks, is reached. This length is narrow and winding and can be dangerous to navigate. When the Severn was busy with tankers carrying petroleum, look-outs always had to be on the bows on this stretch between the parting and the lock.

Originally a staircase lock but now one lock, **Gloucester Lock** was operational by 1812, allowing craft to use the basin at **Gloucester Docks** which was established some years earlier. In 1793, the building of a canal between Gloucester and Berkeley Pill, on the Severn, had been authorised by Act of Parliament but work stopped on the canal in 1799 and did not resume until 1817. By this time, it was decided that the canal should join the Severn at Sharpness and in 1827 the Gloucester & Sharpness Canal was completed. The canal bypassed the narrow, twisting section of the river below Gloucester, making it easier for sea-going craft to reach the city. After the opening of the canal, trade soon flourished, with Irish corn, Baltic timber and French and Portuguese wines being carried to the docks in a variety of tall-masted craft.

At the beginning of the 20th century both sailing vessels and steamers used the docks but decline in business set in as merchant ships became too big for the canal. Trade picked up in the 1920s when tankers started to carry petroleum from Avonmouth to Gloucester but by the 1980s commercial traffic had practically ceased. No longer needed to store merchandise, the tall, brick warehouses, bordering Gloucester Docks have been renovated and some are used as offices and museums. The demise of trading vessels on the Severn and canal means that the berths in the docks are now mainly filled with pleasure craft. However, with the gulls crying overhead, there is still the atmosphere of a sea-port and visitors now come to the docks to sample the delights of the National Waterways Museum, the restaurants and shops and perhaps to take a boat trip either along the canal or river.

The winding Severn leaves Gloucester passing Stonebench, near Elmore and Minsterworth, places renowned as viewpoints for the spectacular Severn Bore, the natural phenomenon of waves sweeping upstream, the largest of which occurs at the time of the February-April and the August-October spring tides. Widening out below Sharpness, then narrowing again at Aust, the river is crossed by the 1966 suspension bridge now carrying the M48. Downriver is the last bridge over the Severn and the longest river crossing in Britain. Known as the Second Severn Crossing, it was opened in 1996 and carries the M4. The Severn now becomes a broad estuary, with the second highest tidal range in the world, flowing on into the Bristol Channel and, eventually, the Atlantic Ocean.

Shrewsbury

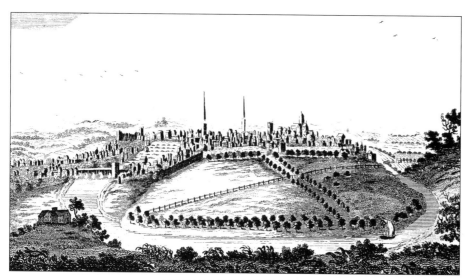

1 *Top left*. Old prints depict Shrewsbury, standing on rising ground, on a peninsula formed by a loop of the Severn. This south-west view, dating from around 1800, presents an impressive sight of the town with its lofty spires and towers.

2 *Middle left*. Shrewsbury Castle and Public School, *c*.1790s. This is one of the illustrations by Samuel Ireland which appear in Thomas Harral's *Picturesque Views of the Severn* (1824). Shrewsbury Castle was built during Norman times by Roger de Montgomery, the 1st Earl of Shrewsbury, on the narrow strip of land at the neck of the peninsula. In the time of Henry II, it became a royal fortress under the custody of a constable and continued as such until the reign of Elizabeth I. During the Civil War, the castle was garrisoned for the king but it surrendered to the Parliamentarians in 1645. Later it was converted into a private residence by Thomas Telford. It now contains the Shropshire Regimental Museum. Shrewsbury School, founded in the reign of Edward VI, was once situated near the castle. In 1882, the school moved to Kingsland and the building became a library and museum.

3 *Bottom left*. The medieval Welsh Bridge was located a little way upriver from the present bridge which replaced it in 1795. Thomas Harral gave this description of the structure in *Picturesque Views of the Severn*:

The old Welch bridge, represented in the annexed view, was anciently regarded as the chief architectural ornament of Shrewsbury. It consisted of seven arches; its extremities were protected by fine castelled gates; and it constituted, in ruder times, one of the most important defences of the town ... The gate at the north-west end, on the Welch side of the river, was secured by a strong outwork; and, in view of guarding the ford below, the battlements, in that direction, had been carried to a great height, and pierced with loop-holes. Over the gate was a massive square tower, with machicolated battlements, the chamber of which was, in modern periods of our history, appropriated as a military guard-house. The tower was taken down about the year 1770.

4 *Below*. The five-arched Welsh Bridge, which after two centuries is still in use today, was built by John Carline and John Tilley. Boatmen used the middle arch when navigating the river while a small arch on the west side went across the towing-path.

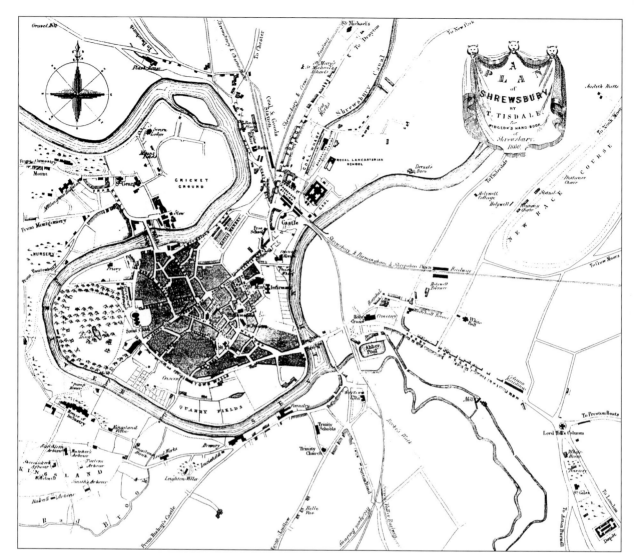

5 *Above*. This plan of Shrewsbury was drawn by T. Tisdale for Henry Pidgeon's *Handbook of Shrewsbury* (1860). Besides the Welsh Bridge, the English Bridge and Shrewsbury Railway Station Bridge, there were three ferries at this time. Since then, Port Hill Footbridge (1922), Kingsland Toll Bridge (1881) and Greyfriars Footbridge (1879) have been built across the Severn between the Welsh Bridge and the English Bridge and the ferries are no more. The plan shows the Quarry, a splendid riverside park, which for many years has been the venue of the world-famous Shrewsbury Flower Show.

6 *Above right*. Port Hill Footbridge and the *Boat House Hotel*, c.1920s. Port Hill Footbridge, connecting the Quarry with Frankwell, was designed by David Rowell & Company of Westminster and paid for by the Shropshire Horticultural Society. The half-timbered *Boat House Hotel* was used to house plague sufferers in the 17th century and later became an inn frequented by boatmen. In this view there are pleasure boats for hire on the hotel's river frontage and an advertisement for W. & J. Abley, boatbuilders.

7 *Right*. Opposite the main avenue of the Quarry stands the picturesque boathouse of the Pengwerne Boat Club which had a fleet of pleasure and racing craft. The bridge crossing the river is the wrought-iron Kingsland Toll Bridge.

8 *Above left*. Steam-powered pleasure boats on the river below Shrewsbury School, *c*.1910. The Severn surrounds the town in the shape of a horseshoe and was safe for pleasure boating between the Welsh Bridge and the English Bridge, boats and punts being available for hire by the hour or the day. A favourite afternoon trip that took in picturesque and wooded scenery was upstream to Berwick Hall and the Isle.

9 *Left*. A ferry operated from the Quarry to the Kingsland bank and Shrewsbury School's boathouse. The latter was erected as a memorial to a former old boy of the school who died in the First World War.

10 *Above*. This 1905 view of Shrewsbury, from the Kingsland bank, shows part of the Quarry with St Chad's Church on the far left. To the right are the spires of St Mary's and St Alkmund's and the tower of St Julian's Church. The ferry-boat is in the foreground of the picture. At the top of the steps is the ferry mooring post. A replica now stands in its place.

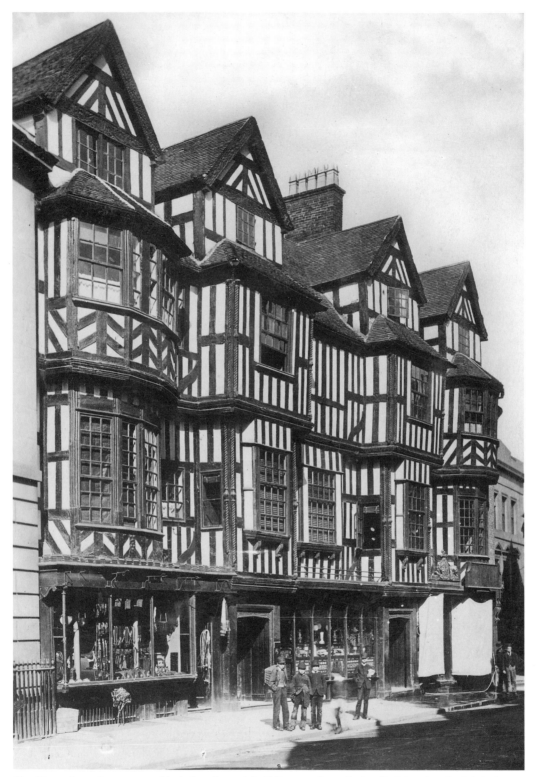

11 Shrewsbury has many old timber-framed buildings such as Ireland's Mansion in High Street. Henry Pidgeon described this Elizabethan house as:

formerly the town residence of the ancient family of Ireland, long seated at Albrighton. It is a spacious half-timbered building, four stories high, finished with gables, on the beams of which are the armorial bearings—three fleurs de lis, three, two and one. The front consists of four ranges of bay windows, the original entrance having been in the centre. The house was built about 1570. It is now divided into three dwellings.

12 The gables of the four-storied Rowley's Mansion appear behind the timber-framed buildings in this turn-of-the-century photograph. Henry Pidgeon commented on the mansion, built in 1618 by draper, William Rowley, as being 'picturesque in its gables and architectural design, and said to be the first brick structure erected in Shrewsbury'. The author added: 'It is now used as a general store-house, and presents a striking picture of "some banquet hall deserted." In the rear are extensive malthouses, of ancient and curious timber-work'. The timber-framed building next to the mansion was once occupied by the draper. It is now a museum known as Rowley's House.

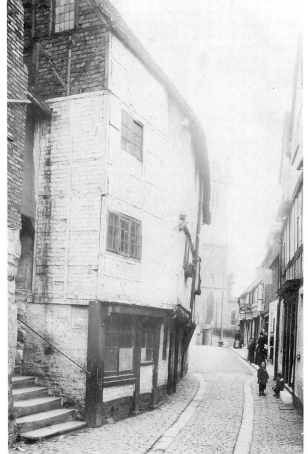

13 Fish Street, c.1907. Between the 14th and 19th centuries, fish were sold here from stalls in the street until the General Market was opened in 1869. On the right, in the background of this view, is the *Three Fishes Inn*. St Julian's Church, one of the town's four old parish churches, is just beyond the inn.

14 Pride Hill, *c*.1911. This has long been one of Shrewsbury's main streets for shopping. It is named after the Pride family whose residence, according to Henry Pidgeon, stood on the western side at the top of the street.

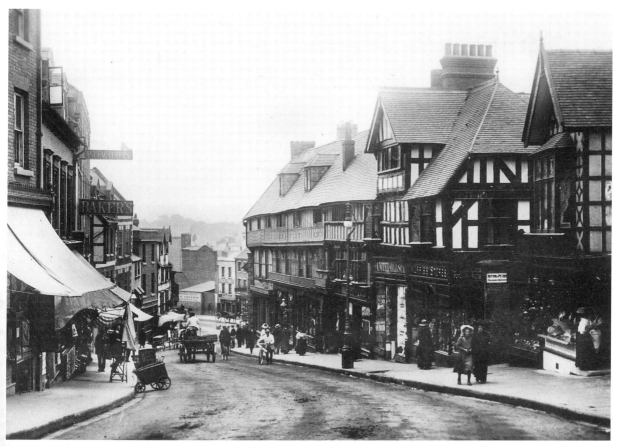

15 Wyle Cop, *c*.1911. There are a number of distinctive, black-and-white buildings bordering this steep hill which leads down to the English Bridge. Henry Pidgeon noted: 'the name is derived from Wyle, a bank or declivity; Cop, the top, or ridge of the bank'.

16 The medieval English Bridge, on the eastern side of Shrewsbury, near the abbey, had both a gateway and a drawbridge but was narrow in width. In 1768, John Gwynne designed a bridge to replace it, the new bridge being opened in 1774. This illustration of the 18th-century structure comes from *Picturesque Views of the Severn* in which Thomas Harral commented: 'To allow a free passage to the frequent floods of the Severn, the architect found himself under the necessity of giving a quicker curve to the bridge than the eye of taste, or a sense of comfort could justify'. The central navigation arch, at 60ft. in width and 40ft. in height from the low-water mark, gave the bridge a definite 'hump' which, though allowing sailing boats to pass beneath, meant a steep slope for horse-drawn traffic on the bridge itself. In the mid-1920s the bridge was rebuilt using much of the original facing stone and decoration. It was opened in August 1927 and looks very similar to its predecessor, except that it is wider and the gradient is much less steep.

Uffington

17 This riverside scene at Uffington was drawn around 1844. Behind the village is the wooded Haughmond Hill, referred to as 'yon bosky hill' in William Shakespeare's *King Henry VI*, Act V. For many years Shrewsbury folk came to the hill for weekend picnics and some locals still remember that crowning its summit was a castellated tower which, by the 1930s, had fallen down. In times past, Uffington had a ferry. After walking through the meadows, the young Wilfred Owen and his family used the ferry to reach the village's small, mid-19th-century church for Sunday services. One occasion, when boots were covered with golden pollen-dust from a field of buttercups, was stored in the poet's memory and woven into one of his First World War poems.

18 The ferryman and presumably his family, in their Sunday best, posed for the photographer in this view of Uffington ferry, dating from c.1910. Rollers, on vertical bars, were used to guide the ferry along the rope in times of strong flow on the river.

Preston Boats

19 Thought to date from Saxon times, the fish-weir at Preston Boats was the last of its kind on the Severn, being in use until 1910 when it was severely damaged by floods. The weir, with its framework of oak piles, cross beams and wattle panels, was breached by three high doorways. Using the ladders alongside the doorways, the fishing nets were lowered and raised from the tops of these structures. Boats passing fish-weirs used a specially-made channel called a 'barge gutter' but difficulties were still encountered, in particular during dry periods. Brian Waters in *Severn Stream* (1949) mentioned a bargeman called Willcocks who, in 1839, uprooted the weir stakes at Preston Boats so that his vessel could pass. He was sued by the fish-weir's owner, the judgement going against him.

Atcham

20 Replacing a 16th-century bridge built by Sir Rowland Hill, the elegant, seven-arched, stone bridge at Atcham, pictured here, was completed by John Gwynne in 1776. This, in turn, was superseded by a ferro-concrete bridge built between 1927 and 1929 to carry the busy A5 across the river. Just downstream of the old bridge stands a red sandstone church, said to be the only church in the country dedicated to St Eata, who lived during Saxon times. Some of the masonry in the building dates from this period when stones from the nearby ruined Roman town of Viroconium were used.

21 The Severn looks tranquil in this view downriver from Atcham Bridge but there are times when it is fast-flowing and dangerous and the fields in this locality are flooded.

Cound

22 Thomas Harral included this print of the Wrekin from Cound Park in his *Picturesque Views of the Severn* and noted: ' From Cound Hall, at Cressage Bridge, and at Sheinton, nine miles, by the road, from Shrewsbury, on the right bank of the stream, the Wrekin forms a fine and conspicuous object in the view'.

Buildwas

23 Another print from *Picturesque Views of the Severn* shows the medieval bridge at Buildwas being repaired in the early 1790s. Concerning this bridge, Thomas Harral remarked: 'From the narrowness of its arches it greatly obstructed the navigation of the river; and although the accident of its destruction, by a high flood, in the year 1795, subjected the county to the expense of a new bridge, the consequent advantage has been great'. In 1796, Thomas Telford used cast iron for the replacement and this was superseded by a further bridge in 1905. The present bridge was constructed in 1992.

Coalbrookdale

24 The Albert Edward Bridge, which crosses the Severn between Buildwas and Ironbridge, was named after Queen Victoria's eldest son who later became King Edward VII. Designed by John Fowler, the cast-iron railway bridge was built by the Coalbrookdale Company and opened in 1864. It is very similar to the Victoria Bridge, near Arley, on the Severn Valley Railway, which was cast and erected by the same company in 1861. John Randall, in his *Handbook to the Severn Valley Railway* (1863), imparted the following information about Coalbrookdale:

> At the foot of Benthall Edge, the Wellington and Severn Junction railway crosses the river by a bridge 200 feet in span, and brings before us, at a glance, this interesting little valley, with its church, its schools and its palatial-looking Library and Scientific Institution. The name has long been famous, as well for its romantic scenery as for its ironworks.

25 Coalbrookdale, a narrow valley running north from the Severn, is renowned on account of Abraham Darby and the Coalbrookdale Company. Another famous person linked with the area was Matthew Webb, the first man to swim the English Channel. A memorial to him is in Coalbrookdale church.

Ironbridge

26 A square-rigged, shallow-draughted, upriver trow is moored above the Iron Bridge in this late 19th-century view, its open hold covered. Upriver trows traded on the river above Gloucester and were smaller than those which worked the Severn estuary and Bristol Channel. It is many years since boats traded to Ironbridge and even further upstream to Shrewsbury and Pool Quay, below Welshpool. The last barge came downriver from Ironbridge to Bridgnorth in 1895 and sank after hitting one of the piers of Bridgnorth Bridge.

27 The road which borders the river between Coalbrookdale and the Iron Bridge is known as the Wharfage. There was a quay here, bordered by warehouses, before the road was built. John Randall noted the sheer height of Lincoln Hill, above the Wharfage, in his *Handbook to the Severn Valley Railway* : 'Underneath the lofty ridge of limestone, the higher portion of which is planted with fir and other trees, are extensive caverns, which are open to visitors, who will find these fossiliferous rocks, rising immediately from beneath the coal measures, highly instructive'. Limekilns can be seen above the houses to the right of this view.

28 Flood at the Wharfage, 4 January 1925. The Severn was, and still is, prone to flooding, with the water sometimes rising to over 12 feet. In the days of trows and barges, however, the summer water level was often too low for navigation and the watermen had to wait for a 'flush' or a 'fresh' to come downriver before being able to leave Ironbridge. When this rise in the water level occurred, many vessels would leave at the same time, which must have been a spectacular sight.

29 Ironbridge, from the Benthall bank, *c*.1920s. In this photograph, the *Tontine Hotel* can be seen at the end of the bridge. St Luke's Church is behind the hotel, on the hillside. John Randall, in *The Severn Valley* (1882), noted:

Strangers arriving at Ironbridge station, which is on the opposite side the river to that on which the town is situated, are often struck with its situation and picturesque appearance, a large proportion of the houses, like Malvern, rising one above the other on the slope.

30 The Benthall bank from Ironbridge, *c.*1920s. Across the bridge, on the southern bank of the river, a steep hill leads to Benthall and Broseley. In this view, Iron Bridge and Broseley station on the Severn Valley Railway can clearly be seen at the foot of the slope. The site of the station is now a car park, convenient for visitors to the Iron Bridge.

31 Ironbridge, *c.*1920s. The bridge with its toll-house is in the left foreground of this view while in the centre is the Square with its shops. A variety of houses and cottages nestle together on the hillside.

32 Tommy Rogers carrying his coracle, early 1900s. Brian Waters in *Severn Stream* related some fascinating anecdotes concerning this celebrated coracle man who had great dexterity when handling his craft. A winner of coracle races, he taught others to coracle and was reputed to have had a prodigious thirst, being able to down many quarts of beer.

33 The trow *William* of Broseley, moored opposite Maw's encaustic tile works at Jackfield, 1880s/90s. Owned by Thomas Beard, *William* was one of the last trows to trade on the upper part of the Severn. During the latter part of the 19th century there were five trows called *William* working on the river, which must have caused some confusion.

Coalport

34 The Coalport ferry, between Coalport and the Werps, was connected by a chain from the top of the mast to the bank and used the flow of the river to cross from side to side. The ferry-boat, with the addition of a rear cabin, may have been adapted from a redundant trow. This photograph, dating from c.1900-10, shows the ferry-boat under repair with the deck removed. The ferry was replaced by the Jackfield War Memorial Bridge, for pedestrians, built in 1922.

35 Advertisement for Coalport Porcelain Works, 1882. In his *Handbook to the Severn Valley Railway*, John Randall noted:

The China Works are about five minutes' walk from the station; they are extensive, and were established during the latter half of the last century, at which time they were removed here from Caughley. The productions are of high order of merit, and combine those distinctive characters for which Caughley and Nantgarw were celebrated. They were successful, some years ago, in obtaining a medal awarded by the Society of Arts; in obtaining a First Class Exhibition Medal in 1851, also in 1855, and again in 1862. The works are very advantageously situated, having the river, the canal, and two railways adjoining.

Bridgnorth

36 The river's approach to Bridgnorth is under an impressive sandstone rock. This view, looking upstream, dates from Victorian times when tourists were recommended to visit the High Rock as its elevated position commanded a good view of hills such as the Wrekin, the Brown and Titterstone Clees and, further afield, the Malverns.

37 This 19th-century view of Bridgnorth from the High Rock shows High Town, standing on the top of a red sandstone cliff, and Low Town along the riverside. Gazetteers once termed Bridgnorth 'The English Jerusalem' while some likened the location to Gibraltar. Visitors to the town today may perceive a definite continental character about the place.

38 A Victorian panorama of Bridgnorth from St James', showing High Town on a plateau, with the church of St Mary Magdalene and the remains of the castle at one end and St Leonard's Church at the other. Castle Walk, along the edge of the town's defences, can also be seen. Charles I, on a visit to Bridgnorth, pronounced this promenade to be the finest in his kingdom.

39 The view from Castle Walk, *c.*1920s. Over the centuries, Bridgnorth Bridge has been much rebuilt. In past times it carried a chapel, dedicated to St Osyth, which was removed in the 16th century. Rebuilt, then widened during the first quarter of the 19th century, the bridge was widened once more in 1960.

40 The church of St Mary Magdalene was designed by Thomas Telford. It was built in 1792, at a cost of £6,000 on the site of an earlier church which had been attached to the castle. Near the church, and leaning at an angle, is part of the keep tower of Bridgnorth Castle, the only remains of the Norman fortification.

41 The old church of St Leonard was damaged during the Civil War. It was rebuilt in Victorian times by public subscription and donations. Dating from 1639, the brick building, next to the church, once housed the Grammar School which was first established nearby in the 16th century. This institution was moved to other premises in 1909.

42 *Right*. The North Gate, *c*.1912. There were originally five gates in the town's defences but the North Gate is the only one left. In 1740, it was enclosed in brick and further rebuilt in 1910. Today, Bridgnorth Museum is in the room above the arches.

43 *Below*. High Street and Town Hall, *c*.1912. The old town hall, which stood outside the North Gate, was pulled down in July 1645 during the Civil War. After the conflict, the present town hall was erected, the stone arches being set up in the summer of 1650 and the timber-framed building constructed on them during July and August 1652. On the right of this view is the mid-17th-century, timber-framed *Swan Inn* which was formerly a coaching inn.

44 *Right*. High Town and Low Town are connected by narrow flights of steps, cut deep in to the sandstone. The Stoneway Steps are pictured here. This steep alleyway of 185 steps has cast-iron kerbs and wrought-iron wall braces which are locally called Pope's spectacles after the works where they were made. The steps were once used by donkeys transporting goods in wicker panniers from the riverside to High Town, coal being among the commodities carried. In his address on 'Bygone Traffic on the Severn with special reference to The Port of Bridgnorth' (1935), Dr. W. Watkins-Pitchford mentioned that the donkeys were still being worked in 1880 and that Richard Dukes, from the Cartway, may have been the last operator.

45 Bridgnorth Lift, *c.*1909. High Town and Low Town are also linked by a cliff railway known as the Lift whose steep, 217-ft. incline rises just over nine feet in every 12 feet. In the early 1930s, W. Byford-Jones, writing as 'Quaestor', featured the lift in one of his articles for the Wolverhampton newspaper, the *Express & Star*. This was later included in a book, *Both Sides of the Severn*. 'Quaestor' found that it cost two pence to go up in the Lift but only one penny to go down, the reason being that the Lift needed more ballast to ascend than to descend. He noted that the train driver knew how many passengers were coming up by the number of rings the girl at the bottom ticket office made on her bell. Then, on a gauge, the train driver would measure the necessary ballast of water into the tank underneath the train to descend. 'Quaestor' remarked on the traditional rivalry that was said to exist between High Town and Low Town. He was told that, although it was true that more Low Towners went up in the Lift than High Towners came down, all those living up the top had to come down in the end, as the cemetery was in Low Town!

46 The Castle Hill Railway and Lift can be seen in the background of this old postcard view of the bridge from Low Town. The quay alongside Underhill Street, at the foot of the bridge, was the main place where goods were landed in the days of the barge trade. Steps to the water's edge can be seen, as can the iron rings in the piers of the bridge to which craft were once moored. Facing the quay, the brick-built house, with window architraves and symmetrical windows either side of the doorway, was at one time occupied by the river steward who overlooked operations on the quay. Ridley's warehouse, at the bridge-foot on the upstream side, had a hoist above a door fronting on to the river so that merchandise could be raised up from boats straight into the premises.

47 Before 1786, when the New Road was built, the only thoroughfare for wheeled traffic, between High Town and the river wharves and Low Town, was the steep and narrow Cartway, part of which can be seen here by the three-gabled, half-timbered Bishop Percy's House. Richard Forester or Forster, a Severn trader, built the house in 1580 and the nearby wharf was named Foster's Loade after him. Other wharves further upstream were known as Skinner's Loade and Friar's Loade.

48 Bishop Percy's House, situated on the Cartway, survived the fire of 1646 during which other timber-framed houses in Bridgnorth were destroyed. It is named after the Rev. Dr. Percy who was born here in 1729. Educated at the Grammar School, Bridgnorth and at Oxford, Dr. Percy was appointed chaplain to George III and later became Bishop of Dromore. He is remembered as being the publisher of some rare, old English ballads, *Reliques of Ancient English Poetry*, which became known as the 'Percy Relics'. John Randall, in *The Tourist's Guide to Bridgnorth* (1875), remarked: 'The doctor kept back a goodly number which he deemed too coarse for publication; but these have since been printed for private circulation'.

49 Bridgnorth station is now the northern terminus of the preserved Severn Valley Railway which runs from Kidderminster to Bridgnorth. The original line, opened in 1862, once ran through a tunnel under High Town before carrying on to Ironbridge and Shrewsbury. John Randall, in his *Handbook to the Severn Valley Railway*, observed: 'The station, at the southern termination of the tunnel, is a chaste building of freestone, and forms an additional ornament to the town'. The same author, in *The Severn Valley*, noted: 'The first object, however, likely to strike the eye of visitors by rail on alighting upon the platform, is a smooth grass-covered mound in front of them, called Pam-pudding Hill, which to strangers, and even local historians, is little better than a puzzle'. Over the years, various theories have been put forward concerning the hill. Some have said that it may have been an Iron Age hill fort while others have supported the idea that it was a Roman camp or a Saxon fortification.

Quatford

50 A print from *Picturesque Views of the Severn* looking downriver and showing Quatford church. Thomas Harral commented: 'The rocky bank, which rises with grandeur almost approaching to sublimity from the Severn side, the solitary church on the eminence, and the surrounding beautiful combination of sylvan scenery, render this spot peculiarly deserving of notice'. There is a legend about the church, dating from Norman times, concerning Adeliza, the second wife of Roger de Montgomery, the Earl of Shrewsbury, who was caught in a violent storm when crossing the sea from France. A priest in her retinue had a dream in which he was told that if his mistress wanted to be saved from shipwreck and see her husband she should make a vow to build a church at the spot where she would meet him. In the dream, the location, a hollow oak where wild pigs sheltered, was specified, as was the saint, Mary Magdalene, to whom the church was to be dedicated. The countess vowed to comply and sure enough the tempest subsided and she later met her husband, at Quatford, at the very spot indicated in the vision. A church in honour of St Mary Magdalene was duly erected, though little of the Norman building remains in the church standing here today.

51 This view of Quatford, looking upriver, dates from 1873. John Randall, in *The Tourist's Guide to Bridgnorth*, gave the following description of the locality: 'Nestling amid trees, embowered in woodbines, perched upon rocks, peeping from upland swells, neat cottages, substantial homesteads, and buildings of different kinds, combine to form a picture pleasing to the eye and suggestive to the mind'. Visitors to Quatford would have noted the ferry. According to John Randall, among the old endowments of Quatford church was 'a piece of land, called Paradise, containing four acres and three quarters, and a house and garden, let at a low rent of 10s. per annum, on condition that the tenant performs the service gratuitously of rowing over at all times the parishioners to the parish church'.

Hampton Loade

52 Lode or loade is derived from a Saxon word meaning a ford. The name, used at a number of places on the Severn, indicates that there was an ancient river crossing in the vicinity. At Hampton Loade, the ferry has long since taken the place of the ford. Joyce Cooper gave her personal recollections of the ferry in 'Severn Ferries' in *Alveley Historical Transactions 1995*. In her account, she mentioned Mr. Bill Parkes who had an eventful time during his years as ferryman from 1942 to 1957 and who lived to tell the tale after his ferry was swept downriver when the Severn rose in August 1957. On this occasion, a partly-submerged tree trunk hit the ferry-boat, breaking the overhead cable. The ferry, carrying Mr. Parkes, went lower in the water as it sailed downstream and, despite attempts to save him by other craft, the ferryman was clinging to the mast, waist-high in water, when the boat reached Arley. The Arley ferry was launched and luckily those manning it were able to catch hold of Mr. Parkes when his boat collided with Arley's larger ferry-boat. The Hampton Loade ferry-boat carried on down to Bewdley where it was eventually retrieved. Taken back upriver, it lay on the river bank while decisions were made about getting a new boat.

53 Hampton Loade ferry still survives, one of the few left on the waterway, despite a fatal accident in December 1964 when the son of the ferryman drowned after the cable broke and the ferry-boat was swept away. Until recently, the ferry was run by Mrs. Annie James and her sister, Mrs. Kathy Evans, but it is now operated by Mr. Darren Page.

Highley

54 *Above*. Coal was struck at Highley in 1879, the mine employing between 400 and 500 men during the years up to 1939 when extraction from the Highley shaft ceased. In 1935-7, a new shaft was sunk at Alveley across the river. Designed by B.R.P. Engineering Co., the Alveley Colliery Bridge was built of concrete during 1936-7, to connect the new colliery with the railway sidings on the Highley side of the river. The Highley miners also used it to reach the Alveley workings. Bill Morgan, who started work at Highley Colliery in 1931, aged 14, recalled the time before the bridge was built in 'Memories' in *Alveley Historical Society Transactions 1996*. Then, Alveley miners who worked at Highley had to cross the river by ferry at Potter's Loade. The ferry-boat took nine or ten people. In times of flood, the going was rough and the boat had to make its way diagonally across the river with everyone using a paddle. During low water a rope was used, the ferry-boat being pulled hand over hand across the river. There was another way of getting to the other side in the days before the bridge was built. Brian Waters, in *Severn Stream*, mentioned that three of the miners crossed the river by coracle, spurning the use of the ferry-boat.

55 *Above right*. This view shows the Highley ferry-boat, several punts and the ferry-rope across the river. During the summer of 1997, the remains of the boat were to be seen sunk at the water's edge in front of the riverside cottages near the *Ship Inn*.

56 *Below right*. The *Ship Inn* is situated close to Highley station on the Severn Valley Railway. It is no wonder that the local folk do not want the return of boats to this part of the river as the location is so idyllic. However, in past times, there was much barge traffic at Highley with craft loading coal, timber and stone. According to Brian Waters in *Severn Stream*, a business of cutting grindstones belonged to a one-time landlord of the inn while stone was cut for some of Worcester's buildings at a quarry half a mile downriver. The *Ship Inn* is mentioned in the same book in connection with the coracle poachers who used to 'kip down for a week' in front of the premises. Night lines would be laid in the river and then the poachers would set about catching roosting pheasants using long poles with wires fixed on the ends. When daybreak came, the poachers would lift their lines and bag up their catch which would be taken away via the convenient railway, the wily hunters returning to the riverside before nightfall.

Upper Arley

57 *Left*. For centuries there was a ferry at Upper Arley. Mrs. Berkeley, in her paper 'The Ferries of Worcestershire' (1931), noted an early reference to it in the Close Rolls for 1323-7, where mention is made of 'the Ferry and the whole wood within the bounds of the chase of Edmund de Mortimer, Earl of Wyre'. The ferry-boat was once pulled across the river using a rope but later became a current-propelled ferry using the rudder to control its course. H.W. Gwilliam, in *Severn Ferries and Fords in Worcestershire* (1982), commented that the ferry was in the possession of the lords of the manor until 1931, when it was made over to the County Council. In the old days, the ferryman was kept very busy carrying over carts and wagons. Foot passengers paid one half penny each but the fare rose to one penny in the early 1930s, though children and churchgoers were allowed to travel free. In the 1940s, fares for motor vehicles were 1s. for a car, 6d. for a motor-cycle and 9d. for a motor-cycle with sidecar. When the ferry-boat, having rotted, became unusable in 1945, two wooden, army landing-craft were used until a new ferry-boat was put into operation on 24 June 1952. By the mid-1960s, the ferry was running at a loss and was closed. It was later replaced by a footbridge. The ferry-boat ended up being moored at Bewdley where it remained for many years. However, in 1996, after severe flood damage, the vessel was eventually demolished.

58 *Below left*. John Randall, in his *Handbook to the Severn Valley Railway*, made these observations about Upper Arley: 'Its ferry on the river, its timbered cottages, partially concealed in green indentations of the hill, its grey church tower and those of the castle near, are a picture of themselves; but when showers of blossoms crown the orchard trees in spring, or ruddy fruits hang ripe in autumn, the scene is more enchanting still'. This view, dating from *c*.1910, besides showing the position of ferry, church and castle, features the *Valentia Hotel* on the extreme left. Pleasure boats are moored to the landing stage as Upper Arley was a popular location for visitors who came by train to enjoy the riverside.

59 *Below*. Arley Castle, which incorporated the old mansion of the Lyttleton family, was rebuilt in medieval style, during the early 1840s, by the 2nd Earl of Mountnorris. In the days of Lord Mountnorris, surprise firework parties were staged at night in the grounds. Once a landmark on the eastern bank of the Severn, the castle no longer exists today.

60 Railway travellers used the ferry to cross the river to reach Arley station, situated on the western bank. Now, passengers on the Severn Valley Railway and visitors to Arley station use the footbridge which was built in 1971.

61 Downstream from Arley, the Severn Valley Railway crosses the river by the Victoria Bridge. Designed by John Fowler, the iron bridge was cast by the Coalbrookdale Company and erected in 1861.

Dowles Bridge

62 Dowles Bridge, *c.*1901. This bridge, built in 1864, carried the railway line from Bewdley to Tenbury Wells, Leominster and Ludlow. The iron spans, which were removed during the 1960s, rested on piers built of stone and blue bricks which are still standing.

63 Dowles ford can be seen in the foreground of this view which looks south from Dowles Bridge. Writing in the late 19th century, George Thompson remarked in *Country Rambles Round Kidderminster*, that barges on the river had been slowly diminishing since the coming of the railways and, as there were no funds from tolls to pay for the removal of shoals, then the passage was silting up and becoming dangerous. He added: 'This is most noticeable at Dowles Ford, where an island of gravel has accumulated and blocked the stream, causing all boats to hug the Wribbenhall side'.

Bewdley

64 *Above.* Thomas Harral included this print of the old bridge at Bewdley in his *Picturesque Views of the Severn* with the comment:

> On the western pier of the centre arch, is seen a wooden gate-house, the end of which, towards the north, served as a residence for the toll-gatherer, whilst that towards the south, commonly called the Bridge-house, was used as the corporate prison.

65 *Right.* Bewdley Bridge, *c.*1910. The old bridge collapsed in the floods of 1795 and was replaced by a new structure which Thomas Harral described as being 'of elegant proportions, exhibiting a light and graceful appearance, superior even to that of Worcester'. This bridge, designed by Thomas Telford, is still in use today. It was erected a short distance upriver from the site of the old bridge in order to line up with Load Street, and opened in 1801. There was a toll-house on the Wribbenhall side, tolls being charged until 1834 when the bridge was free of debt.

66 *Above*. An early photograph of a narrowboat at Severnside North before the quay wall was constructed. This boat was probably based on the canal system as it was of a slightly different design from the 'longboats' or 'Severners' which traded on the river. 'Severners' had deeper hulls than canal narrowboats, enabling them to carry cargoes of up to 33 tons compared with the canal boat tonnage of 23 tons.

67 *Left*. Severnside North was also known as Coles Quay, possibly because coal transported by river was once unloaded here. This photograph, dating from *c*.1914, shows that pleasure boats were then using the quay where W.R. Bell advertised boats for hire from the *George Hotel* landing stage. On the latter, there are two more advertisements, one a poster about day excursions by river to Stourport and Holt Fleet, the other a board announcing that a large boat would be running to Arley. Among the pleasure boats of the time were the horse-drawn *Fairy Queen* and *Arley Castle*. Further along the quay, the sign for the *Old Mug House* is just discernible. It was at this inn that the watermen used to seal bargains with a mug of ale. Opposite the quay can be seen the floating swimming baths, built on a base of two narrowboats, while in the far distance is Dowles Bridge.

68 *Below left*. The landing stages, adapted from narrowboats, rode high on the swollen river at Severnside North and the water reached the doorsteps of the houses further along the quay during the flood in December 1910.

69 *Below*. The X on this old postcard of Bewdley's waterfront indicates the spot where a fatal accident occurred on 12 June 1910. An account of the incident is related on the back of the postcard: 'A pony, attached to a trap containing a man, his mother, wife and little boy, took fright and ran straight for the river. The man fell out before it reached the water but the others fell into the river with the pony and trap. They were all taken out but the old lady died afterwards'. The rescuers, Benjamin Bishop, Harry Postins and Mr. Ainsworth, were later awarded certificates from the Royal Humane Society at a ceremony attended by Mr. Stanley Baldwin, M.P.

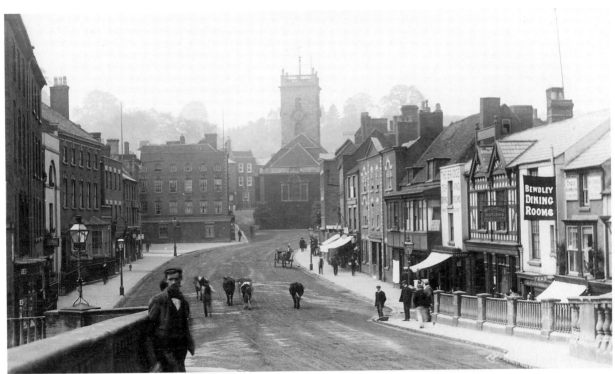

70 Load Street, looking west from the bridge, *c.*1910. This wide street, bordered by an interesting variety of buildings, runs from the bridge to St Anne's Church which dates from 1745-8, though the tower is earlier, having been erected in 1695-6. The large Georgian house, near the church and facing the bridge, is now the Midland Bank. On the right, next to the Bewdley Dining Rooms, was the half-timbered *Angel Inn* where Charles I stayed in June 1645 after being defeated at the Battle of Naseby. The inn has been rebuilt, a little way back from the street, since this photograph was taken.

71 Load Street, looking east to Bewdley Bridge, *c.*1917. On the left is the *George Hotel*, a former coaching inn, which was well-patronised during the 18th and 19th centuries. When this view was taken, the hotel advertised carriages for hire and a motor garage.

72 High Street, *c.*1905. Bewdley once had a great number of hostelries but the demise of the town's river trade led to the reduction in the number of public houses. I.L. Wedley, in *Bewdley and its surroundings* (1914), noted: 'something like fifty having been closed since the days of the Reform Bill'. The *King's Head*, on the left of this view, was still in operation during the early years of the 20th century but today is no longer an inn.

Wribbenhall

73 The riverside quays and their blend of 17th- and 18th-century buildings are among the most impressive features of both Bewdley and Wribbenhall, harking back to the days when river trade brought prosperity to the locality. Beale's Corner is shown in this view of Wribbenhall, taken from the Bewdley side. Some say that it was named after the Beale family, who, in past times, owned the nearby property, while others say it was originally called Bale's Corner because bales of wool or other goods were once unloaded here. In the background is Wribbenhall House, demolished many years ago, while the *Black Boy Inn*, just visible opposite, still stands. Beyond the four-storied building, on the corner, is an opening between the houses named Pewterers' Alley. Along it, the pewter manufacture was carried out for which Wribbenhall was well-known. On the right of Beale's Corner, there was once a timber-framed warehouse belonging to the pewtersmith, Benjamin Cotterell, but by the time this photograph was taken it had been altered.

74 Local lads posed for the photographer at Beale's Corner during the December floods in 1910.

75 The floods had receded slightly at Wribbenhall when this photograph was taken in December 1910.

76 This old postcard shows a narrowboat either loading or unloading timber at Wribbenhall. The boatmen were forced to use very long gangplanks because of the shallowness of the river at its summer level. The boat may have belonged to Thomas Gardner, a coal and timber merchant of Severn Side South. Nowadays, a narrowboat upriver of Stourport is a very rare sight, the normal limit of navigation being at Gladder Brook, a short distance above Stourport Bridge.

Blackstone Rock

77 Downstream from Bewdley, the Severn sweeps around the bold, jutting-out Blackstone Rock. Caves here, known as the Hermitage, feature in a legend concerning a knight who married a lady much younger than himself. Soon tiring of her company, he left her in the charge of one of his pages while he went away for long periods. Falling in love and being fearful of the knight finding out, the young pair fled, seeking refuge in Bewdley, a sanctuary town. The husband came after them but at the old chapel on the bridge he was refused entrance to the town. Biding his time, the knight watched and waited until one day the lovers crossed the bridge and he confronted them. A sword fight ensued which ended when the lady darted between the opponents and received a fatal blow, whereupon the adversaries left the spot in some haste. Many years later, at Blackstone Rock, a palmer, thought to have just returned from the Holy Land, took up residence as a hermit, hewing a chapel and living quarters for himself out of the rock. During the years that followed, he was looked upon as a holy man and people came to him for guidance and the forgiveness of their sins. One day a stranger begged to be given absolution for an act he had committed long ago. On hearing the visitor's sorrowful tale, the hermit perceived that he was none other than his one-time page. Masking his emotions, he advocated that the penitent should leave the dark cave and make his confession in the light of heaven, so they both walked to the top of the cliff. Suddenly, as the man pleaded to be forgiven, the hermit grabbed him and made himself known to his enemy. During the fight which followed, they lurched backwards and forwards over the sheer drop of the Blackstone Rock, until at last, grappling together, they pitched into the river and were swallowed up by a whirlpool below the cliff.

Ribbesford

78 St Leonard's Church, Ribbesford, *c*.1917. After being struck by lightning, the church was restored in the late 1870s to the disgust of John Ruskin who would have liked the old building to remain peacefully as it was on the banks of the Severn. Ribbesford church has a number of interesting features, among them the Norman tympanum over the north doorway. This semi-circular stone, between the door and the arch, has an unusual carving said to represent an archer knight of the locality who, when out hunting, aimed at a deer but shot a salmon that sprang from the river at that moment. In the churchyard, the inscriptions on some of the gravestones are an indication of the close proximity of the river. The epitaph to boatman John Oakes, who died in 1821, reads:

> Boreas' blast and Neptune's waves
> Have tossed me to and fro:
> I strove all I could my life to save:
> At last I obliged to go.
> Now at anchor here I lay
> Where's many of the fleet;
> But now once more must I set sail
> My Saviour Christ to meet.

Areley Kings

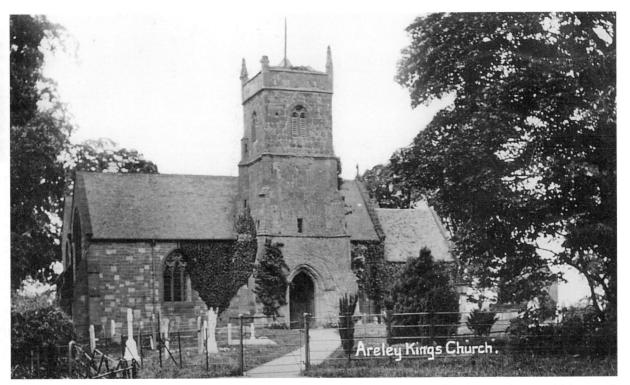

79 St Bartholomew's Church, Areley Kings, *c*.1914. This church, rebuilt by F. Preedy in 1885-6, is set on high ground, overlooking the Severn. The base of the Norman font has an inscription concerning Layamon who was priest at Earnley-by-Severn, now thought to be Areley Kings. Layamon, who died in 1200, was the author of *Brut*, one of the first poems in English. It is said that he wrote this chronicle of British history at the Redstone Rock hermitage, downriver from Areley Kings.

Stourport-on-Severn

80 *Left*. The first bridge at Stourport was a three-arched structure of local sandstone. It was opened in 1775, replacing the ancient ford and ferry at Redstone, a short distance downstream.

81 *Below*. In the late 18th century, Stourport Bridge was damaged by floods and was superseded in 1806 by a single-arched, iron bridge which, in turn, was replaced by the present bridge. The latter, pictured here in *c*.1913, was completed in 1870 and is still in use today. On the extreme right of this view is Stourport's floating swimming bath which was opened on 13 August 1879.

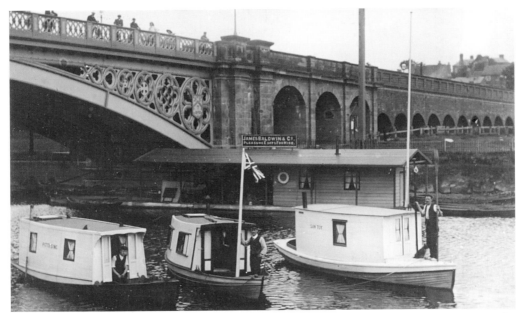

82 *Above*. The pleasure boat business of James Baldwin & Co. was established in 1865 and its landing stage was the first below Stourport Bridge. Advertisements, dating from 1907, show that houseboats, skiffs, canoes and sailing boats were offered for hire with special catering for camping parties. At this time, river trips by motor-launch for small private parties of up to 12 people could be obtained, while private boats were built to order and stored.

83 *Above*. Bridge Street, looking down to Stourport Bridge. The drapery store, on the left, was situated on the corner of Bridge Street and York Street. Today, Bridge Street is much busier with traffic than in this peaceful scene dating from the early years of the 20th century.

84 *Above*. High Street continues north from Bridge Street. This view of the shop-lined street dates from *c*.1914. I.L. Wedley, in *Old Stourport* (1912), commented: 'High-street is wonderfully altered. The old stone steps leading to the shops are taken away and all down the street new windows and brilliant lights seem to have been put in everywhere'.

85 *Left*. Taking steamer trips on the Severn was a favourite pastime in the early years of the century. In this view of Stourport's riverside, *Beatrice* is making her way downstream to Holt Fleet. On the left is the *Crown*, a hotel popular with holidaymakers, while on the right is the canal bridge near the junction of the Staffordshire & Worcestershire Canal with the Severn. The Riverside Café was situated opposite Stourport Boat Club.

86 Stourport Boat Club, *c.*1911. In the mid-19th century, the pioneers of boating and racing at Stourport were a group of young men called the Blue Caps who bought an old boat, described by I.L.Wedley as 'a tub, heavy, with narrow-bladed oars and hard-fixed seats'. Later came the renowned Red Caps who rowed in Stourport's regattas and had a great deal of success.

87 The *Tontine* was built by the Canal Company, the many-roomed hotel being opened in 1788. During the first half of the 19th century, the hotel was much in demand for social occasions but by the 1880s, with river and canal trade in decline, the *Tontine* had undergone a change. John Randall, in *The Severn Valley*, wrote:

> Railways have robbed the Severn and the canal of the traffic, which now passes by instead of into its commodious basins. We found the Company's great commercial hotel, the *Tontine*, a large square block, with rooms sufficient to make up a hundred beds, and equally extensive stabling, diminished to proportions of one of the smallest inns in the town, its extensive rooms being let off to form dwelling houses.

88 This Stourport quayside scene was photographed *c.*1914. The *Dove*, a narrowboat, or 'longboat' as they were known on the Severn, had just left the canal locks and drifted around the steamers behind it. A boatman supervised the operation from the bank while the horse waited patiently behind the girl dressed in white. The boat, belonging to James Dudfield of Tirley, was a 'Severner', designed for work on the river as well as on the narrow canals. It differed from other canal narrowboats as it had a more bluff bow, fitted with two large timberheads for towing by steamers. The cargo it carried was probably coal as the boat was not fully sheeted up; only the side-cloths had been used to keep water out of the hold.

89 The steam tug *Athlete* can be seen between the trow *Taff* and a 'Severner'. Referring to the decline in canal and river trade, John Randall, in *The Severn Valley*, remarked on an occasion when this tug left Stourport: 'One solitary barge, loaded with sand from the neighbourhood, bound for Newport, was all that the *Athlete*, capable of tugging a hundred such, could muster on the Monday morning we went on board, a short time ago; true it took others in tow between there and Gloucester'.

90 A 'Severner' lay alongside the trow *Leader* as cargo was transhipped between the two boats. They were moored to the quay at Stourport, between the two sets of locks. The pleasure steamer in the background was the *May Queen*, operated by Captain Harry Hatton of the *Angel Hotel*, Severnside. The captain also operated other vessels. In 1907, he was advertising steamer trips on the *Lady Honor* and *Bonavista*, starting from the *Angel Hotel* and going from Stourport to Holt Fleet, twice daily after Whit Monday. Special parties up to 180 were catered for and there were refreshments on board.

91 The Shropshire, Worcestershire and Staffordshire Power Station was opened on 2 June 1927 by the Prime Minister, Mr. Stanley Baldwin, who once lived at Wilden House and later at Astley Hall, across the river. At the opening ceremony, he told those assembled that when he was young he had played cricket on the field where the power station now stood. A number of important people came from London by special train for the inauguration and on that day crowds of children lined Vale Road. The brick-built power station took 240 million gallons each day from the River Stour and discharged into the Severn. Noted for its seven chimneys and its unusual façade, the power station was closed in 1983 and has since been demolished.

92 In 1800, a horse towing-path was completed between Bewdley and Coalbrookdale. It was extended from Bewdley to Worcester in the first years of the 19th century. This view of a horse-drawn narrowboat below Stourport dates from *c.*1906. The narrowboat was being towed on a long, cotton line which was attached to a tall mast erected alongside the boat's normal towing mast. The extra length of the tall mast stopped the line drooping in the water. It also enabled the line to clear the bankside vegetation which could snag it and thus pull the horse backwards into the river.

Redstone Rock

93 A short distance downstream of Stourport, on the west bank of the Severn, is a red sandstone cliff known as Redstone Rock. In the past, the ancient river crossing nearby was important as it linked the old road from Wales to London. Hermits, living in the caves at Redstone Rock, are said to have kept the ferry and to have charged a good deal for its use. When the water was low enough, the ford just below the ferry was used. Tradition maintains that, after his death at Ludlow Castle in 1502, the body of Prince Arthur, son of Henry VII, was carried across this ford on its way to Worcester Cathedral for interment. When Stourport Bridge was opened, in 1775, the ferry lost its custom.

94 Caves at Redstone Rock once formed a hermitage with a series of rooms and a chapel. In the 16th century, Bishop Latimer of Worcester noted that the caves were 'able to lodge 500 men and as ready to lodge thieves as true men. I would not have hermits masters of such dens'. During the three centuries after the dissolution of the monasteries, the hermitage was used for a variety of purposes including a school and an ale-house besides providing dwellings. By the late 19th century, the caves were deserted according to George Thompson, in *Country Rambles Round Kidderminster*, who wrote that the dwellings 'being deemed both unsafe and insanitary, were condemned, and are now tenantless'.

Lincomb Lock and weir

95 Lincomb Lock, the northernmost lock of the six locks on the Severn, was completed in 1844. This view, dating from *c*.1914, shows the weir on the left, the 'lock island' with the lock-keeper's house and the 100-ft. lock. The steam tug *Athlete* was waiting for narrowboats, just discernible by the smoke from their cabin chimneys, which were descending in the lock.

96 Lincomb weir, *c*.1912. The 300-ft. weir at Lincomb was built in 1843. Its construction, combined with the rise in water level above the weir and the excavation of the river bed during 1842-4, brought about the demise of the two nearby fords, Redstone ford and Cloath or Cloth House ford.

The Burf

97 Although it looks peaceful enough here, the ferry crossing at *Hampstall Hotel*, at the Burf, could be hazardous. In fact, the sign above the landing stage once read, 'Passengers cross here at their own risk'. An accident on 4 August 1919 illustrated the danger of overloading the ferry-boat. The boat should have accommodated only 10 people but there were 17 aboard on that fateful day. When water came over the side, the boat overturned and nine of the passengers were drowned.

Lenchford

98 Mrs. Berkeley, in 'The Ferries of Worcestershire', noted that the ferry at Lenchford was worked by the landlord of the *Lenchford Inn* for the convenience of his customers but was not for the use of the general public. There were also wharves at Lenchford, one being for the private use of Witley Court. This must have been busy in past times, as it was here that coal, brought by water, was unloaded for the great house. Apparently, farm tenants were required to cart coal on a daily basis to the Court as part of their rent agreement.

Holt Fleet

99 *Above left*. Like Lincomb Lock, Holt Fleet Lock was completed in 1844 and shared the same dimensions of 100ft. by 20ft. This view of the lock dates from *c*.1918.

100 *Left*. There was a ferry at Holt Fleet long before Thomas Telford's bridge was opened in 1828. For many years previously, the inn here had catered for ferry travellers. In Victorian times, after improvements to the river had been made, the old alehouse and its tea gardens became a major riverside attraction.

101 *Above*. Hordes of day trippers from the Black Country used combined, rail-and-river tickets to visit Holt Fleet by steamer and, by 1910, the *Holt Fleet Hotel* was advertised as having 'accommodation for 500 for dinners, luncheons and teas'. Sadly, the old Georgian building was pulled down in the 1930s and its replacement compares unfavourably with the original inn.

102 This photograph records an occasion in the early years of the 20th century when over 2,000 lamperns were caught at the waters of the *Holt Fleet Hotel*. In past times, lamperns or river lampreys, being tasty and boneless, were thought to be a great delicacy. These eel-like fish are grey with cream-coloured undersides and may grow to around 20 inches, being as thick as a man's thumb. When adult, lamperns live in the sea, but may come upriver at any time between the autumn and the following spring, spawning in May or June. The young lamperns stay in fresh water for up to five years after which they migrate to the sea becoming parasites on other fish. Lamperns were trapped in a similar way to eels by using putcheons, tall baskets made out of osiers which were placed in the river.

Holt

103 Downriver from Holt Fleet, and overlooking the Severn is Holt Castle, with its square, 14th-century tower and battlemented mansion house which dates from the 15th century.

104　Bevere Island, the second largest of the Severn's natural islets, is renowned in the history of Worcester as a refuge for the city's Saxon inhabitants when the Danes came in 1041. In the 17th century, folk crowded here again to escape the plague; hence the lower end of the island was often referred to as Camp. An iron footbridge connects the island to the riverside. Bevere Lock, once known as Camp Lock, adjoins the island. The lock, measuring 100ft. by 20ft., and the 300-ft. weir were built on a shoal of gravel, the work being completed in 1844.

105 Below Camp Lock, a boating party paused to have a photograph taken at the landing stage of the *Camp House Inn*, c.1911.

106 The *Camp House Inn*, c.1910. According to Mrs. Berkeley, in 'The Ferries of Worcestershire', a punt ferry was used here, as a rope could not be stretched across the river on account of the steamer traffic. The landlord of the inn gave Mrs. Berkeley information about the establishment when it was used by boatmen. Then, stabling for a horse, mule or donkey cost 3d. per night. Looking back further to the days of the bow-hauliers who pulled the trows, the landlord spoke about the victuals supplied to them. These comprised twopenny worth of bread and cheese each day and cheap cider or beer which cost a shilling for five pints. An ounce and a half of tobacco was also provided.

107 Kepax ferry was located at Barbourne, on the outskirts of Worcester, a short distance from the old tower belonging to Worcester Waterworks. H.W. Gwilliam, in *Severn Ferries and Fords in Worcestershire*, noted that the ferry was also called 'Bailey's Boat' after Mr. Bailey, the ferryman.

108 The Dog and Duck ferry, *c.*1908. This well-used ferry was situated in a very picturesque spot, opposite Pitchcroft, with steps leading up from the landing stage. The ferryman's house was once an inn called the *Dog and Duck*, the name deriving from the pastime of putting ducks with clipped wings on the river and unleashing dogs to catch them. The location was also a wharf, in times gone by, and goods were taken up the steep slope by donkeys.

109 This view of the *Grandstand Hotel*, *c.*1913, is looking upstream with Pitchcroft on the right bank. Here, horse-racing started in the early 18th century. There was once a ferry in the vicinity called the Grandstand ferry but it no longer operates. Likewise, the original grandstand and the hotel are no more.

110 *Above*. Worcester's first railway bridge over the Severn, carrying the Worcester and Hereford Railway, was erected in 1860. On its completion, government inspectors found a fault in the two cast-iron, arched spans and the bridge was declared unsafe until the defect was corrected. In 1904, this bridge was superseded by the girder bridge, shown here, which used the original abutments and the central support. The new bridge was designed by the Great Western Railway's chief engineer, J.C. Ingles. The railway engine, beneath the bridge in this photograph, stands on the Butts siding which extended as far as the South Quay, downstream of Worcester Bridge. A trow can be seen tied up to the wharf, on the opposite bank, by J. Wilesmith's timber yard.

111 *Left*. Upstream of the present-day bridge, there was once a medieval bridge, demolished after the construction of Worcester Bridge, shown here. Designed by John Gwynne and completed in 1781, the cost of building the new bridge was almost £30,000. Two circular, domed toll-houses were erected on the west side of the bridge and tolls were originally levied on both foot passengers and vehicles. Since it was built, the bridge has been widened several times and there was major reconstruction work in the early 1930s.

112 *Above*. The trow *Hastings*, owned by the Droitwich Salt Company, at Worcester Bridge during the 1883 floods. These small trows, known as 'Wich barges', were used to carry salt from the workings at Droitwich along the Droitwich Barge Canal and down the Severn for transhipment at Gloucester.

113 *Above right*. Worcester Electric Tramway Siege, 1903. During 1903-4, the tramway system in Worcester was electrified. Horse tram-lines were taken up and replaced by lines with a 3ft. 6in. gauge, the work causing great upheaval in the city centre. This time of disruption was known as the 'Worcester Electric Tramway Siege' and was commemorated by a set of postcards, one of which is shown here. In this view, the tram-lines are being laid across Worcester Bridge.

114 *Right*. For many years, High Street has been regarded as Worcester's main street for shopping. It also houses the Guildhall, the city's chief civic building, which is thought to be one of the finest town halls in the country. This splendid edifice, with its carved pediment, was probably designed by Thomas White and built between 1721-3, replacing the original, timber-framed Guildhall.

115 *Above*. This busy street scene at The Cross, looking towards the Foregate railway bridge, dates from *c*.1915 when horse-drawn vehicles were much in evidence. An electric tram is in the centre background, the electric tram service having been inaugurated on 6 February 1904. The tower of St Nicholas' Church dominates the area and a variety of shops can be seen including Cassidy's, the jewellers, below the clock on the left.

116 *Right*. In past times, the Cornmarket was both a centre of commerce and a place where punishments were meted out. The stocks and pillory once stood here and the public came to watch transgressors being whipped. Shops in this view, dating from *c*.1915, include pawnbrokers, Joseph Coleman Ltd. and Webbs Cash Furnishing Stores, on the left, with Richardson's grocery and Brown's drapery on the right. The half-timbered building in the centre is known as King Charles' House.

117 *Above right*. King Charles' House was once part of a three-storied mansion and is named after Charles II who lodged here before the Battle of Worcester in 1651. After his defeat, he is said to have escaped by the back door just as his enemies were arriving at the front entrance. This old postcard dates from the first decade of the 20th century, the notice above the door advertising the occupancy of Charles Collins, bricklayer.

118 *Left*. This view of Friar Street shows an enchanting variety of old buildings, many of which date from the 15th and 16th centuries. Greyfriars, the fine, timber-framed building on the left, was built *c*.1480. When this photograph was taken, *c*.1915, part of it housed an antique shop. Now, Greyfriars has been restored and is administered by the National Trust.

119 *Below left*. Below Worcester Bridge is South Quay and, a little further along the riverside, Worcester Cathedral. This view shows many interesting features of the locality. These include the warehouses operated by the hop and seed merchants, Firkins & Co. and the tall chimney belonging to the glove factory of Dent, Allcroft & Co., besides the spire of St Andrew's Church, known as 'Glovers' Needle', and the cathedral. A railway wagon stands on Butts siding which terminated on South Quay. It had been hoped that there could be a link to Diglis Dock but the cathedral authorities refused permission for the line to go past the cathedral. Among the pleasure steamers along the quayside is *Holt Castle*, moored in front of the Severn Iron Warehouse.

120 *Below*. The heyday of the Worcester pleasure steamers was between the 1880s and the 1920s, when regular trips ran upriver to Holt Fleet and Stourport and downriver to Tewkesbury. *Holt Castle* belonged to the Castle Line of steamers, owned in 1910 by Mrs. Roberts and operated from South Quay. This vessel had accommodation for 326 passengers and at that time was the largest steamer on the river. The other steamers in the fleet were *Avonmore Castle*, capable of carrying 320, and the smaller *Hanley Castle* which only carried 50 passengers.

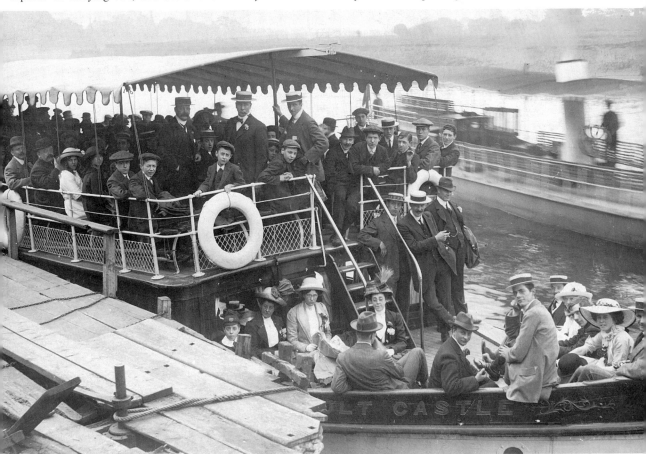

121 This composition of cathedral, riverside promenade and ferry must have gladdened the eye of many a photographer. Dating from 1084, the earliest part of Worcester Cathedral is the crypt, built by Bishop Wulstan. The imposing tower was built in the 14th century. Among the many interesting features of the cathedral is the circular chapter house and the tomb of King John, who died in 1216. A ferry was operated from the Watergate and originally used by the monks to reach their land on the Severn's western bank. In later times, the white-and-green ferry-boat was called *Betty* after a former boatwoman who kept the ferry for many years in the latter half of the 19th century. Although the ferry stopped working during the 1950s, in recent years it has been re-established.

122 Diglis Locks were completed in 1844 with the smaller lock having the same measurements as those upstream and the larger lock being 150ft. by 30ft. There were two locks instead of one as river traffic was once busy here with the junction of the Worcester & Birmingham Canal just above the locks.

Powick

123 A short distance below Diglis Locks, the River Teme joins the Severn. Powick Bridge over the Teme was the setting for a cavalry encounter in 1642 at the start of the Civil War. The final engagement of the conflict, the 1651 Battle of Worcester, also took place in the vicinity on land near the confluence of the two rivers.

The Ketch

124 Passenger steamer at the *Ketch Inn*, *c*.1914. During the 19th century there were pleasure grounds here which were well-frequented and a ferry once plied across the river from the inn taking passengers bound for the village of Powick. The *Ketch Inn* is named after a type of sailing vessel. John Randall made this comment about the name in *The Severn Valley*:

Below Worcester, at the head of the lake is the Ketch, but why or wherefore so called we could not ascertain; the version given by the captain of our vessel, that it was 'where they ketched the king, who had been hiding in the woods', cannot be a satisfactory solution. All we know is that the little alehouse there was wont to catch a good many customers.

Kempsey

125 At one time there were a number of fine residences in the vicinity of Kempsey but some are now long gone. These thatched cottages in Church Street were among the humbler dwellings and are typical of the black-and-white houses associated with many Worcestershire villages.

126 The half-timbered building between the brick-built dwellings was once the village school. Later, it housed the caretaker of the village hall before being demolished in 1961.

Pixham

127 In past days, Pixham ferry was a vehicle ferry used frequently by members of the hunt and their foxhounds. Mrs. Berkeley commented on the crossing in 'The Ferries of Worcestershire'. At this time, there was no road to the ferry but access to it could be gained across Kempsey Ham. Mrs. Berkeley had misgivings about travelling across this huge field in the dark, especially as she had noted some posts here and there marked 'Danger' and a steep slope to the ferry. In the early 1930s, it cost 2d. for foot passengers, 3d. for a bicycle and 1s. for a motor vehicle to cross the river. The vehicle ferry was operated until the late 1930s when the ferry-boat fell into disrepair. According to L. Richardson, in *The River Severn between Upper Arley (Worcs.) and Gloucester* (1964), a smaller ferry-boat was used until 1947, the year when a great flood occurred. After the demise of this boat, the ferry was not reinstated.

Severn Stoke

128 Severn Bank, a castellated mansion, overlooks the river a short distance from the village of Severn Stoke. This early 20th-century view shows the two-storied side of the house with its iron veranda. The other side is three-storied and gives the impression of a tower.

Hanley Castle

129 A little way downriver, on the opposite bank, is a late 17th-century house, Severn End, the ancestral home of the Lechmere family. After much of the building was destroyed during a fire in 1896, it was rebuilt in its former style. This photograph of the house dates from *c*.1909.

Upton upon Severn

130 There have been a number of bridges at Upton upon Severn, from a wooden structure in the late 15th century and a red sandstone bridge in the 17th, to the present crossing made of steel and built at the beginning of the Second World War. In between, a bridge was built in 1854 which included a drawbridge. This was replaced by a swing bridge at the Upton end in 1883, at a cost of about £1,500. Upstream of the bridge was the landing stage for passenger steamers.

131 Water has risen up to the sides of the old bridge in this view of winter floods which possibly dates from 1911. The onlookers were keeping dry though the owners of the bicycles probably had wet feet! In the background is the *King's Head*. Signs advertising the *White Swan Inn*, the *Star Hotel*, the *White Lion* and the *Bell* can also be seen.

132 Another way to travel during the floods was by punt. This photograph was taken looking upstream, the flood water covering the road to Hanley Castle, on the left.

133 *Top*. Steam tug *Victor*, owned by the Severn & Canal Carrying Company, passing Upton Bridge, with a trow and several narrowboats in tow. Founded in 1874, the company provided a regular towing service for their own and for other traders' vessels. During the summer, when the current was slower, a tug could tow up to 12 narrowboats. *Victor* was built by G.K. Stothert and Company at Bristol in 1904. At first, the four-man crew was made up of captain, engineer, mate and fireman but later it was reduced to three.

134 *Above*. The *King's Head*, at one end of the 19th-century bridge. Many inns were to be found in Upton upon Severn, a reminder of the days when the town was a thriving inland port.

135 *Above right*. Church Street, *c*.1920s. In Georgian times, the medieval church at Upton was pulled down and replaced, its tower being retained and crowned with an eye-catching cupola designed by Anthony Keck. In 1879, when a new place of worship was built for the town, this church near the river was abandoned. Today, only the tower, locally called 'the Pepperpot', remains, the nave having been demolished in 1937.

136 *Right*. The churchyard is on the right of this view of High Street, dating from the early years of the 20th century. On the left, at the corner with Dunn's Lane, stands the *Star Hotel*, once a coaching inn, while the *Anchor Inn* is the half-timbered building on the opposite corner of the lane. The latter inn is featured in a tale of body snatching. It was from here, in 1831, that two bodies, exhumed from the churchyard at Hanley Castle, were dispatched in packing cases to London for medical research.

137 Old Street, looking towards the Square, *c.*1920s. Horse-drawn and two-wheeled transport are prominent in this Upton street scene. In the background is the *White Lion*, a former posting house, made famous in Henry Fielding's *Tom Jones* (1749). The inn has another claim to fame in this epitaph of one of its landlords, though no gravestone survives:

> Here lies the landlord of the Lion,
> Who died in lively hopes of Zion;
> His son keeps on the business still,
> Resigned unto the heavenly will.

Uckinghall

138 Uckinghall Cross, *c.*1910. In past times, wayside crosses were set up at crossroads or where roads forked. Since the Reformation, many crosses have disappeared and those that remain are often damaged. Travellers to Uckinghall ferry, the last in Worcestershire, would pass this broken cross on their way to the river.

Ripple

139 Set further back from the river than Uckinghall is another village possessing a cross. Ripple is described by John Randall, in *The Severn Valley*, as a 'neat but straggling village, linked to its churchyard by an elegant octagonal cross, denuded of its limbs, and those primitive institutions, the parish stocks and public whipping post, overlooked by good-looking almshouses bearing the name of their founder'.

Tewkesbury

140 The steep cliff at the Mythe, near Tewkesbury, is noted as a habitat for woad, a rare plant growing to about four feet, its yellow flowers appearing in July and August. A blue dye, obtained from the leaves, was used both in ancient times and in later centuries.

141 Mythe Bridge, *c.*1916. Designed by Thomas Telford and opened in 1826, Mythe Bridge, with its 170-ft. iron span, carries the Tewkesbury to Ledbury road across the Severn. Telford remarked that the bridge was the handsomest that had been built under his direction. Noted for the high arches in its abutments which permit the passage of flood water, Mythe Bridge cost £36,000 and was originally a toll-bridge.

142 The steam-powered Borough Flour Mill, situated on the Old Avon at Tewkesbury, a short distance from the confluence of the Severn and Avon, was built in 1865 by Samuel Healing, on the site of a mill which had existed in the 13th century. Now known as Healing's Mill, it was extended in 1889 and again in 1935, the establishment changing over to electric power in the 1950s. In 1976-7 the interior was modernised but the interesting 19th-century exterior was retained. During recent years, grain has been carried to the mill by the motor barges, *Tirley* and *Chaceley*, two of the last cargo-carrying craft on the river.

143 Judging by the number of servicemen and nurses aboard *S.S. King*, moored on the Old Avon, this photograph was taken at the time of the First World War. *King* was the largest in the fleet of four passenger steamers owned by Charles Bathurst whose boatyard was situated on the Avon with access to the Old Avon and the Severn. At 71ft. 6ins. in length and built of teak throughout, the steamer was licensed to carry 192 passengers and had an 80 h.p. engine by T.A. Savery & Son. In later years, cladding was fitted and *King* was turned into a houseboat. Discovered at Welsh Back in Bristol during December 1995 and purchased by a group of enthusiasts, *King* is undergoing major restoration work at present.

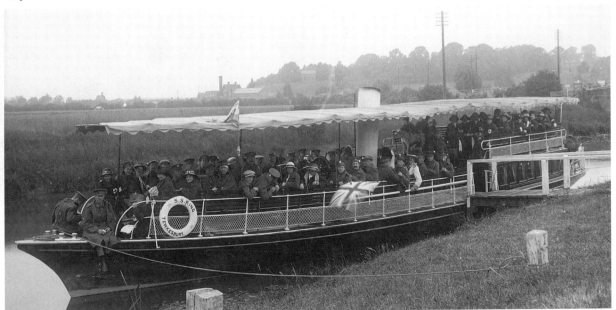

144 *Above left*. A rare photograph, taken at Avon Lock, Tewkesbury, *c.*1875, of *Bee*, the last steam barge to trade between Gloucester and Evesham. In *Waterways to Stratford* (1962), Charles Hadfield noted that *Bee* appeared on the Avon in May 1862. Until 1875, when commercial traffic ceased on the Upper Avon, *Bee* carried corn from Gloucester to Lucy's Mill at Stratford but after this date much of her trade was with Evesham. By 1917, most of the mills between Tewkesbury and Evesham had closed down so *Bee* was sold by her owners, J. Rice & Son of Gloucester.

145 *Above*. The *Olde Black Bear Inn*, on the corner of Mythe Road and High Street, in the early years of the 20th century. Traditionally renowned as the oldest inn in Gloucestershire, the building is said to have been established in 1308 though its timber-framing dates mainly from the 16th century. Now, the inn has a garden with moorings on the Avon but when this photograph was taken an adjoining warehouse for beers, wines and spirits stood in the present-day inn's garden.

146 *Left*. The Mill Avon, shown here, was probably cut by the monks of Tewkesbury Abbey during the 12th century to provide water for the abbey mill. In this view, old warehouses and workshops can be seen on the left while on the right is Severn Ham, a flat hay meadow between the Mill Avon and the Severn.

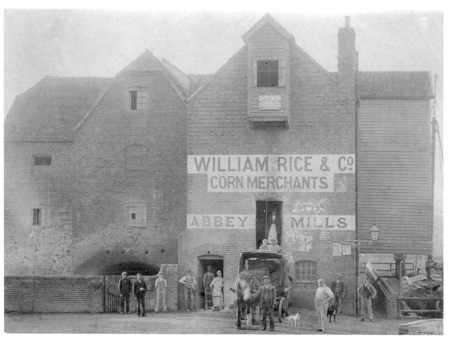

147 The monks of Tewkesbury Abbey worked a mill on this site for centuries. Abbey Mill was rebuilt in 1793 and, at this time, had eight pairs of millstones and four waterwheels. It gained fame as 'Abel Fletcher's Mill' in Mrs. Craik's novel *John Halifax Gentleman* (1856). This early postcard view shows the mill when it was still operated by corn merchants, William Rice & Co. In later years, the premises were used as a café and in recent times the old mill has housed a restaurant.

148 The *Hop Pole Hotel*, on the right in Church Street, was a busy coaching inn during the early 19th century when a number of stage-coaches passed daily through the town. Charles Dickens brought the *Hop Pole* into renown with these words in *The Pickwick Papers* (1837):

At the Hop Pole at Tewkesbury, they stopped to dine; upon which occasion there was more bottled ale, with some more Madeira, and some Port besides; and here the case-bottle was replenished for the fourth time. Under the influence of these combined stimulants, Mr. Pickwick and Mr. Ben Allen fell asleep for thirty miles, while Bob and Mr. Weller sang duets in the dickey.

149   This old postcard shows a busy scene at the upper end of Church Street near the Cross but there is no indication on the back of the card of the event taking place. The variety of interesting buildings shown here includes the twin-gabled *Berkeley Arms*, the fourth building along the street, a timber-framed, three-storied inn which may date back to medieval times.

150   Ladies riding bicycles in Tewkesbury's High Street caused heads to turn when this photograph was taken in Edwardian times. High Street itself has a number of impressive buildings, which, no doubt, have caused many visitors' heads to turn. Among them are half-timbered, jettied buildings such as The House of the Nodding Gables, a little way along the street on the left of this view, and Clarence House, opposite on the right.

151 Tewkesbury has always been prone to flooding. In this view of the June flood of 1924, which covered the Gloucester Road at the southern entrance to the town, the horse and wagon appears to be towing a fire engine.

Upper Lode and Lower Lode

152 This picture of the lock at Upper Lode, Tewkesbury comes from the *Illustrated London News* of 4 September 1858. Details of the improvement to the River Severn navigation and the lock accompanied it:

> The works include a lock 120 feet long by 32 feet wide, with a depth of 32 feet in the chamber, six-feet lift, and a minimum depth of nine feet of water upon the cills. Below the lock is a basin, 180 feet long by 80 feet wide, inclosed by a third pair of gates, which, when used with the upper gates of the lock, converts the whole of the intervening space into one large lock-chamber of 300 feet in length. The object of this arrangement is to pass a steam-tug, with her fleet of vessels, at one locking, thus effecting a great saving of time. The weir, which, with the lock, is constructed in a new channel excavated for the purpose, is 500 feet long, and is built with limestone from the neighbourhood of Chepstow.

The opening of the lock on 10 August 1858 was also reported: 'Half a dozen boats and barges sailed down the old channel, which was then closed: they then passed twice in and out of the lock. Firing of batteries and loud cheers from the assembled multitudes accompanied the opening ceremony'.

153 Before Mythe Bridge was opened, the Severn was crossed by ferries at Upper Lode and Lower Lode. In monastic times, the Lower Lode ferry was used by the monks of Tewkesbury Abbey to reach nearby Forthampton Court which belonged to the abbey. This postcard, dating from *c.*1912, shows the vehicle ferry with punt attached, setting out from the Lower Lode bank. The 15th-century *Lower Lode Hotel* is in the background while one of Bathurst's steamers is moored on the left. In recent years, a ferry for pedestrians and cyclists was re-established, operated by the inn between Easter and September.

Deerhurst

154 The Saxon church at Deerhurst can be seen from the river. Originally belonging to a priory here, the church of St Mary is renowned for its double triangular-headed windows in the nave and for its splendid carved Saxon font.

155 Near St Mary's Church is Odda's Chapel, another building dating from Saxon times. The stone-built chapel is attached to a 16th-century half-timbered house and its true identity was not discovered until 1885 when work was being done on the house. The Latin inscription on a stone found nearby, in the 17th century, recorded that the chapel was erected by Earl Odda in 1056 in honour of the Holy Trinity and for the soul of his brother Aelfric.

Apperley

156 Situated beside a coal wharf, this inn at Apperley is called the *Coal House* and was one of several inns on this stretch of the Severn which catered for the rivermen. When this photograph was taken, the hostelry was known as the *White Lion Inn*.

Haw Bridge

157 The river bank at the *Haw Bridge Inn* is crowded with people but the special event which this Edwardian postcard commemorates is unknown. One arch can be seen of the original three-arched bridge, which once spanned the Severn here. This cast-iron bridge collapsed after the *MV Darleydale* collided with it on the night of 20 December 1958. It was replaced by the present single-span structure.

158 Wainlode Hill rises to a height of nearly 300 feet on the east bank of the river. The river has eroded into the Keuper marls of the hill to form an almost sheer cliff face. Old narrowboats were sunk at the water's edge to try to prevent further erosion. These can be seen today, surrounded by water. Just discernible in the background of this view is one of the Severn & Canal Carrying Company's tugs, with a train of lighters and narrowboats in tow, heading downstream towards Gloucester. The punt in the foreground is typical of the Severn, being used for ferrying people across the river as well as for fishing.

159 Salmon fishing near Wainlode Hill, *c.*1907. In past times, one of the occupations along the Severn below Tewkesbury was long-net fishing for salmon. The net had to be made specially to fit the stretch of river where it was to be employed and a new net had to be made every season, the time taken to knit it being about two months. When the season opened on 2 February a long-net, weighted down by lead sinkers and buoyed up by corks, would be paid out into the river from a punt. Four men were needed to operate the long-net which, having been drawn downriver, was landed at a flake, a wooden stage parallel to the river.

Ashleworth

160 Ashleworth ferry, *c.*1907. A horse ferry was needed at Ashleworth as here the towing-path changed to the east side of the river before carrying on to Gloucester. On the opposite bank from Ashleworth, the road from the former ferry leads to the village of Sandhurst.

161 Ashleworth church and tithe barn, *c.*1912. The church of St Andrew and St Bartholomew stands near the impressive late 15th-century tithe barn. Built of limestone, the barn has a stone slate roof and measures 125ft. by 25ft. A property of the National Trust, it is still in working use.

Maisemore

162 There have been a number of bridges across the Severn's western channel at Maisemore, carrying the road which, on leaving the bridge, approaches Gloucester alongside the flat Maisemore Ham on Alney Island. This print from *Picturesque Views of the Severn* shows the 18th-century structure which was replaced by the present bridge, built in 1956. Maisemore's bridges, over the centuries, have been viewing points for half of the famous Severn Bore, the spectacular series of waves that surge upriver at the time of the spring tides and which are divided at the Lower Parting, the other half sweeping up the eastern channel.

Gloucester

163 Gloucester Cathedral is prominent in this scene from *Picturesque Views of the Severn*, drawn from above the city's Westgate Bridge. Formerly the Benedictine Abbey of St Peter, building work began in 1089 with reconstruction in later centuries.

164 *River Queen*, one of Bathurst's steamers, photographed above Westgate Bridge. Cheap steamer trips were frequently run downriver, during the summer, to Wainlode Hill, Gloucester and Sharpness. Licensed to carry 147 passengers and fitted with an engine by W. Sissons & Co., *River Queen* was 68ft. by 12ft. and built of teak.

165 Gloucester's Westgate Bridge carried the main road out of the city to the west and Wales. The old bridge was much favoured by artists, among them Samuel Ireland whose late 18th-century illustrations were used in *Picturesque Views of the Severn*. Thomas Harral commented:

Since Mr. Ireland visited Gloucester, this bridge, with the fine old embattled gate—the last memorial of the ancient fortifications of the city—having fallen to decay, has been taken down, and the bridge has been replaced with an elegant structure, of a single arch, eighty-seven feet in its span. The new bridge, from a design by Smirke, is of stone from the Forest of Dean, faced with Cornish granite. It connects on the west with a causeway of stone, called Over Causeway, which extends through the low meadows across the Isle of Alney towards Over Bridge.

166 *King*, belonging to Charles Bathurst of Tewkesbury, moored above Robert Smirke's single-arched Westgate Bridge. The bridge was built between 1813-16 and demolished in 1941, a Bailey bridge taking its place. Construction work on the present bridge started in the early 1970s and it was completed in 1974.

167 Over the centuries, Westgate Street was a very busy thoroughfare as it led to Westgate Bridge and the road to Wales. An inn was erected here by St Peter's Abbey, around 1500, to take the overflow from its guesthouse. It later became known as the *Golden Fleece*, an indication of the prominence of the wool trade in Gloucester. By the early 20th century, when this view was taken, the inn was known as the *Fleece Hotel*, a sign for which can be seen on the left-hand side of the street. On the neighbouring premises, the large advertisement for pianos, jutting out over the pavement, belonged to Wallace Harris, of No. 11, who claimed to be 'the largest dealer in Second-Hand Pianos in County' while Rose & Rose, Tailors, who traded at No.13, were also hatters, hosiers and shirtmakers. On the opposite side of the street, among other businesses, is Winfield's Seed Warehouse and the Palace, a picture house advertising film projection daily from 2.30-10.30. The truncated spire of the church of St Nicholas can be seen in the background.

168 Eastgate Street, looking towards The Cross, *c.*1912. For hundreds of years there was a large stone cross at the meeting place of Gloucester's four main streets but this was taken down in the mid-18th century. The tall 15th-century tower at The Cross belonged to the church of St Michael the Archangel, now no longer standing. In days gone by the curfew bell was tolled from its belfry. Although originally not so important as the three other streets, after the railway was opened to the east of Gloucester's centre, Eastgate Street took on a new lease of life, some distinguished buildings being put up here. The impressive portico to Eastgate Market, built in 1856, can be seen on the left-hand side of this view. In the early 1970s, during the development of a new shopping precinct, the portico was moved from its position here and re-erected a short distance along the street.

169 In medieval times, travellers from London and the east of the country came into the city by the North Gate. Some of them would have stayed in Northgate Street at the galleried *New Inn*, built by St Peter's Abbey during the mid-15th century. Said to have had accommodation for over 200 people, the inn was styled 'New' because it was erected at the location of an earlier inn. A sign for the *New Inn Hotel* is on the right-hand side of the street on this postcard dating from *c*.1912.

170 Southgate Street, looking towards The Cross, *c*.1913. The 16th-century gabled building with a timber-framed frontage, on the left of this photograph, is known as Robert Raikes' House. This is because Robert Raikes, one of the founders of the Sunday School movement and publisher of the *Gloucester Journal*, used part of the building as a printing office during the latter half of the 18th century.

171 Crowds gathered to gaze at the subsidence of Gloucester's quay wall, at the entrance to Gloucester Lock, which occurred on 7 September 1912.

172 Warehouses along the eastern side of the Main Basin at Gloucester Docks, viewed from Gloucester Lock, *c.*1913. Most of the brick-built, slate-roofed warehouses were built to store corn and merchants often painted the names of their companies in bold lettering on the warehouses' sides. Philpotts Warehouse, built in 1846, can be seen on the extreme left while Albert Warehouse, erected in 1851, is behind R.D. Petroleum Stores. Albert Warehouse was turned into a flour mill in 1869, ceasing operation in 1977. It now houses the Robert Opie Collection in a museum of advertising and packaging.

173 The Main Basin at Gloucester Docks was busy with trows, narrowboats and a steamship when this photograph was taken in the early years of the 20th century. The trows included the *Waterwitch* of Gloucester, belonging to the Severn & Canal Carrying Company, the *Times* of Bristol and the *George* of Gloucester. Moored against the *Waterwitch* was the narrowboat, *John Gilbert*. Behind the unidentified trow, on the right, was a row of warehouses on the West Quay. These were knocked down in the 1960s. The North Warehouse, in the centre of this picture, was the first warehouse to be constructed in the docks and finished just before the canal opened in 1827. The warehouses of the Severn & Canal Carrying Company can be seen, on the left, standing along the corner of the Main Basin and the Barge Arm. This company, trading between the Bristol Channel ports and the Midlands, was the leading transporter of goods on the Severn, being especially concerned with carrying cocoa beans to the Frampton, Blackpole and Bournville factories of Cadbury's.

174 *Left.* On 24 January 1906, an advertisement appeared in the *Gloucester Citizen* concerning the sailing barque *Success* which had recently arrived in Gloucester Docks. She was billed as the 'World's Most Wonderful Vessel. Original Convict Ship. 116 years old'. Other claims included, 'An Eye-Opener to Prison Reformers ... All Ancient Cells and prisoners represented within them ... 48 years since a Convict trod the Chain-worn Deck'. In fact, these claims were false, the *Success* having been used as an emigrant ship in the late 1840s and early 1850s and a women's prison between 1860 and 1868. Nevertheless, it appears that she drew a considerable number of visitors. The unusual history of this ship is told in Donald Hall's article on 'The chameleon barque *Success*' (1997).

175 *Right.* The trow *Spry*, moored in the Barge Arm at Gloucester Docks in 1997. Originally built at Chepstow in 1894, the *Spry* was completely reconstructed at Ironbridge Gorge Museum in recent years. She was transported by road to Bristol in April 1996 for the International Festival of the Sea and in June of that year took her first trip under sail in the Severn estuary, after which she was towed upriver to Sharpness and along the canal to Gloucester Docks.

176 A passenger steamer, probably *Wave*, making its way from Gloucester Docks along the Gloucester & Sharpness Canal. *Wave* along with *Lapwing* was operated by the Gloucester & Sharpness Steam Packet Co. and there were daily services between Gloucester, Hardwicke, Saul, Frampton and Sharpness throughout the year. The Pillar Warehouse, on Baker's Quay, is the first building on the right while others supported by pillars can be seen in the distance. The erection of pillared warehouses allowed the quayside to be used while goods were lifted out of moored vessels by a winch in the loft.

177 Gloucester viewed from the Severn, two miles below the city. Craft have not needed to use the dangerous, winding section of the tidal river between the city and Sharpness since the completion of the Gloucester & Sharpness Canal in 1827.

Bibliography

Baylis, T.J.S., *Stourport-on-Severn in old picture postcards* (1983)

Baylis, T.J.S., *Discover Stourport-on-Severn* (1987)

Berkeley, Mrs., 'The Ferries of Worcestershire', *Transactions of the Worcestershire Archaeological Society for 1931*, new series, vol.8 (1932)

Bradley, A.G., *A Book of the Severn* (1920)

Bridges, Tim and Mundy, Charles, *Worcester: A Pictorial History* (1996)

Burd, C., *Tewkesbury in old picture postcards volume 2* (1990)

Byford-Jones, W., *Both Sides of the Severn*

Byford-Jones, W., *Midland Leaves* (1934)

Carr, Tony, *Shrewsbury: A Pictorial History* (1994)

Clark, Catherine, *Ironbridge Gorge* (1993)

Conway-Jones, Hugh, *A Guide to Gloucester Docks* (1988)

Conway-Jones, Hugh, *Working Life on Severn & Canal: Reminiscences of Working Boatmen* (1990)

Cooper, Joyce, 'Severn Ferries', *Alveley Historical Society Transactions 1995*

Davis, Susanna, *Bewdley As It Was* (1979)

Drewett, John and Roberts, John, *Midland Rivers* (1966)

Garner, Laurence, *The Visitors' Guide to the Severn and Avon* (1986)

Green, Colin, 'The Severn Trow', *Archive: The Quarterly Journal for British Industrial and Transport History*, Issue 12 (1996)

Grundy, Michael, *Worcester's Memory Lane*, vol.3

Gwilliam, H.W., *Severn Ferries and Fords in Worcestershire* (1982)

Hadfield, Charles, *The Canals of the West Midlands* (1966)

Hadfield, Charles, *Waterways to Stratford* (1962)

Hall, Donald, 'The chameleon barque Success', *Archive: The Quarterly Journal for British Industrial and Transport History*, Issue 13 (1997)

Harral, Thomas, *Picturesque Views of the Severn* (1824)

Haynes, Clive and Malcolm, Old Worcester as seen through the camera (1986)

Haynes, Clive R., *Worcester Within The Walls* (The 'Changing Face of Worcester' Series, 1996)

Hilton, Charles, *Tewkesbury in old picture postcards* (1982)

Hobson, Kenneth and Purcell, Charles and Angela, *Bewdley's Past in Pictures*, vol.1 (1993)

Hurle, Pamela, *Upton: Portrait of a Severnside Town* (1988)

Jenks, Alfred E., *The Staffordshire & Worcestershire Canal* (1907)

Kempsey Collection, (1984)

Kerr, Peter, *Walks Around The Severn Valley* (*Bridgnorth to Stourport on Severn*) (1997)

Kissack, Keith, *The River Severn* (1982)

Jenkins, J. Geraint, *The Coracle* (1988)

Lane, B.A., *Time & Tide Wait for no Man on the Severn* (1993)

Lees-Milne, J., *Worcestershire: A Shell Guide* (1964)

Morgan, Bill, 'Memories', *Alveley Historical Society Transactions 1996*

Morris, Richard K., *Canals of Shropshire* (1991)

Marsh, Jean, *Bewdley a XVth century Sanctuary Town* (1979)

Moore, Ann, *Curiosities of Worcestershire: A County Guide to the Unusual* (1991)

Morris, Richard K., *The Shropshire Severn*

Moss, Philip, *Historic Gloucester* (1993)

Nicholson/Ordnance Survey Guide to the Waterways 2. *Severn, Avon & Birmingham* (1997)

Owen, Brian R., *Worcester in old picture postcards* (1992)

Paget-Tomlinson, E., *Britain's Canal & River Craft* (1979)

Parkhouse, Neil and Pope, Ian, 'Steam Towage on the Severn', *Archive: The Quarterly Journal for British Industrial and Transport History*, Issue 6 (1995)

Pearson, Michael, *Pearson's Canal & River Companion*: *Severn & Avon* (2nd edn., 1990)

Pevsner, Nikolaus, *Worcestershire*, The Buildings of England Series (1968)

Peel, J.H.B., *Portrait of the Severn* (2nd edn. 1980)

Pidgeon, Henry, *An Historical and Illustrated Handbook for the Town of Shrewsbury* (2nd edn., 1866)

Randall, J., *Handbook to the Severn Valley Railway* (1863)

Randall, J., *The Tourist's Guide to Bridgnorth* (1875)

Randall, J., *The Clay Industries including the Fictile & Ceramic Arts on the Banks of the Severn* (1877)

Randall, J., *The Severn Valley* (2nd edn., 1882)

Richardson, L., *The River Severn between Upper Arley (Worcs.) and Gloucester* (1964)

Ross, Kathleen, *The Book of Tewkesbury* (1986)

Rowbotham, F.R., *The Severn and its Bore* (1967)

Russell, Ronald, *Rivers* (1979)

Scorpio, Sam, *Stourport-on-Severn: A Town Walk for Visitors* (1983)

Smith, Peter L., *A Pictorial History of Canal Craft* (1979)

Taylor, John Neufville, *Fishing on the Lower Severn*

The Gentleman's Magazine, xxviii (1758)

Thompson, George, *Country Rambles Round Kidderminster*

Trinder, Barry, *Bridgnorth: A Town Trail & Brief History* (2nd edn.,)

Ware, Michael E., *Britain's Lost Waterways* (vol.2, 1979)

Waters, Brian, *Severn Stream* (1949)

Waters, Brian, *Severn Tide* (2nd edn., 1955)

Watkins-Pitchford, W., 'Bygone Traffic on the Severn with special reference to The Port of Bridgnorth' (address given to the Bridgnorth Historical Society on 11 March 1935)

Wedley, I.L., *Old Stourport* (1912)

Wedley, I.L., *Bewdley and its Surroundings* (1914)

Whitehead, David, *The Book of Worcester* (1976)

Wilding & Son, *Shrewsbury Illustrated: The Official Guide of the Shrewsbury Corporation* (7th edn., 1933)

Witts, Chris, *A Century of Bridges* (1996)

Index

Roman numerals refer to pages in the Introduction, and arabic numerals to individual illustrations.